The Timeshare Coach ^{SM}

Carl Garwood

Grosvenor House
Publishing Limited

This book is published by
Grosvenor House Publishing Ltd
28-30 High Street, Guildford, Surrey, GU1 3HY.
www.grosvenorhousepublishing.co.uk

A CIP record for this book
is available from the British Library

ISBN 978-1-906210-24-3

All Napoleon Hill quotations are used with the permission of the
Napoleon Hill Foundation, One College Avenue, Wise, Virginia 24293,
whose website is www.naphill.org

The Timeshare Coach ^{SM}

CHANGE YOUR THOUGHTS SELL MORE TIMESHARE........FACT

When you read this book, read it as if I am speaking to you and you alone. Read this book as if I am your own personal coach, by your side and motivating you to reach that new level in your Timeshare sales career.

Highlight any sentences, quotations and words that are meaningful to you. Write down any quotations that feel important to you, read them every day until you memorize them.

Re-read certain parts of the book again and again and take all the Timeshare tips that you learn and do the most important thing.

PUT THEM INTO ACTION.

> "What the mind can conceive and believe it can achieve."
> *Napoleon Hill*

To my wife and best friend Caroline and our beautiful twin daughters Chloe Louise and Charlotte Elizabeth. Thank you for your patience while I wrote this. I love you all so much, you make my life complete.

I would like to thank,

Bruce Rohman, for the impact you
have had on my Timeshare Career........................**FACT**

Harald Hasiba, for making me a better
Coach. Harald you are one of the best
leaders I have ever worked with ....**FACT**

Richard Trevithick, for his belief and
support and giving me my first motivational
CD, it changed my life..**FACT**

I would also like to thank the following.
At some time in my career, each has been
My Timeshare Coach..**FACT**

Fred Jones
Julie Bett
Jose Rodrigues
Chris Kemp
Victor Todd
Martin White
Carl Deach
Alan Belcher
John Smart
Neil Scott

CONTENTS

YOUR PERSONAL TIMESHARE COACH. The Timeshare Coach ^{SM} is your strongest believer. He will show you the best in yourself and help you achieve more sales. The Timeshare Coach ^{SM} will give you direction, put purpose in your stride, strengthen your will and give you unquestioned belief. He is your own personal coach.

PART 1

WARM UP

YOUR FIRST THOUGHTS OF THE DAY

WAKE UP. What is the first thing you think about when you wake up in the morning? Is your self talk positive or negative? Put yourself in the position of opportunity. How does the way I wake up affect whether or not I am going to get a sale today? What is the alternative to using positive self talk? It's the best breakfast you can have. Today is your day. **FACT**

MUSIC. What does your mind listen to on your way to work? Music is what feelings sound like. Music is the medicine of the mind. Replace listening to the news with listening to your music. Replace sixty hours a year of negativity with sixty hours of motivation. That's what winners do, why not you?

PART 2

PITCH

TIMESHARE TIPS FOR YOUR TOUR

THE TOUR. Prejudging: To judge beforehand without possessing adequate evidence. How can you have adequate evidence to decide whether the clients you are about to tour will buy or not just by looking at what they wear, or where they come from? Change your thoughts: Sell more Timeshare...... **FACT**.

Prejudging is a word you must take away from your vocabulary.

Superstition is a form of fear; it is also a sign of ignorance. People who succeed keep open minds and are afraid of nothing. Do not let your self talk turn negative, telling you what is going to happen before you have even started. Remember, your thoughts are the only thing of which you have complete control at all times. You have the only audience that gets to pay *after* your performance.

OBJECTIONS. What are objections? If you cannot handle objections then you are in the wrong job......**FACT**

Which sales line do you want to work on? A Timeshare Sales Professional welcomes objections. <u>Agree</u> <u>Confirm</u> <u>Overcome</u>. *"Just so you know, we will not make a decision today."* Don't fight objections, welcome them, and want them.

NEGATIVE PARTS OF THE TOUR. Will I be able to get what I want? Does the maintenance fee go up every year and by how much? Can I sell it? Do not lie to your clients, there is no need to......**FACT**.

Put negatives in, it builds up trust. Ask the right questions. Women decide 92% of the family's vacations. All skills are learnable.

WHY. Ask why, engage your clients; if the client says it then it must be true. **Why** is such an important word. Make a friend, make a sale. You close the client or the client closes you......**FACT**

ASK FOR THE SALE. You have to ask for the sale, not just at the end but throughout the presentation. *"You have done a great job but we need to think about it."* It should always be down to the money. You must price condition. No matter what they say, agree with it. **"No" is Good**

SHORT TOURS. How can you get someone to part with thousands of dollars in less than sixty minutes? Take control, make them earn their gift. Short tours play a big part in the difference between top and bottom performers. Make a friend, make a sale.

CLIENTS OF THE 21ST CENTURY. Rescission period, Cooling off time, Resale companies, The Internet, Neighbours over the garden fence *("What, you bought a Timeshare?")* The image of the Timeshare presentation. There is no need for heat or little white lies.

PART 3

BACK END CLOSING

CONCEIVE, BELIEVE AND ACHIEVE

PMA PERSONAL DEVELOPMENT. Selling Timeshare is like a mental rollercoaster, as many things happen that can take your mind up and then down. Hold a positive attitude at all times. Focus on the **now** not the **then**. Negative people at work. The clients close you or you close them, someone is closing. In this job it's today not yesterday; it's today, it's now. How do you react to situations? You cannot see the picture if you are in the frame. Ways to motivate yourself when the going gets tough. Pain is temporary, quitting is forever. Struggle is good, I want to fly. Personal development and motivation are like nutrition. Persistence is a state of mind, so it can be cultivated. With persistence will come success.

BELIEF. A strong opinion, conviction. How good are you at selling Timeshare? Having confidence and belief plays a very big part in your success in Timeshare Sales. This is because you are giving instructions to the most faithful servant you will ever have, your subconscious mind.

What the mind can conceive and believe it can achieve......**FACT** What are affirmations? I am a fantastic Sales Professional. Thinking. You will achieve your goals........**FACT** Six simple steps. Success. Do or do not, it's your choice.

Act Now, Your Personal Coach. It's up to you. Positive thinking is like golf. The Timeshare Coach ^{SM} is your strongest believer. None of us are Smarter than all of us........**FACT**

As A Man Thinketh

Books for Further Reading

Testimonials

The Timeshare Coach ^{SM} Change Your Thoughts, sell more Timeshare........FACT

A SHORT BOOK THAT YOU CAN READ BETWEEN TOURS, TO CREATE AWARENESS AND KEEP YOU SHARP AND FOCUSED.

The way Timeshare has been sold has changed over the years. The Timeshare Coach ^{SM} shows you that by controlling your thoughts you can sell more Timeshare......**FACT**

Yes you still have to get your clients to want to buy your Timeshare, but you have to adapt your presentation to the clients of the 21st century. Survey Sheets and hard closes do not work anymore. The clients are wise to this and now have Timeshare Laws to protect them. With all these challenges Timeshare as an industry is still growing in sales every year.........**FACT**

You choose the thoughts you hold in your head; they can be positive or negative, never both at the same time.

The Timeshare Coach ^{SM} shares with you how you can maintain a positive attitude and have unquestionable belief in yourself all of the time, no matter what is in front of you or what challenges come your way.

If you sell Timeshare then you will have gone through your training at your resort and know the basics of a warm up, tie downs, 3rd party stories, features and benefits and all the tools that you use to get your clients to want to buy. **TODAY**

The best Sales Professionals have the best product knowledge and the best attitude. This book covers your mental attitude and self talk to give you the belief that there is a sale in every client you see.

The Timeshare Coach ^{SM} shares a simple proven formula that has been used by some of the world's most successful people in the last 100 years and explains how you can adapt this formula to setting your goals to achieve your Timeshare success.

You have the most valuable sale tool on you, it's you, your mind and your thoughts. Control them and feed the right thoughts to your mind and you will sell more Timeshare.

You as a Timeshare Sales Professional are that skilled that you can convert a couple who have no intention of buying.

They are only in front of you because they have been promised a gift if they attend a 90 minute presentation, yet 3 hours later can be spending over $20,000 on a week of Timeshare every year.

THAT'S TALENT

Take that talent and add to it the tips from this book and you can write your own pay check.

Learning to build the best in yourself by learning to give yourself a refreshing new programme of positive self thoughts is one of the greatest gifts you will ever give yourself.

If you sell Timeshare then this book is a must read. Read it, learn from it, re-read it, take the tips, use them and put them into **ACTION........TODAY**

> *"All you are or ever shall become is the result of the use of which you put your mind."*
> *Napoleon Hill*

WAKE UP

WHAT IS THE FIRST THING YOU THINK ABOUT WHEN YOU WAKE UP IN THE MORNING?

Do you want another five minutes sleep?

Do you lie there and hit the snooze button again and again and again?

Are you hung over?

Do you want to go to work?

Apart from your thoughts, preparation is important.

Are your clothes ready?

How long do you give yourself before you have to be out the front door ready for work making sure you are there on time, thinking ahead for traffic or your bus being late?

Do you eat breakfast before you go or is it on the go?

How is your mind? What are your first thoughts?

It has been said that the first few minutes of your day - in what you think and how you behave - determine how the rest of your day will be.

If you are going to change your thoughts and sell more Timeshare then I believe the first step is: how you start your day.

Let's look at the **wrong way** to start your Timeshare successful sales day.

1. **Do not want to go to work?**
   This is a killer right away. If you do not even want to go and sell Timeshare today then stay in bed; with the attitude of not wanting to go work you will just burn your tour. Any objection, any excuse, the slightest thing will set you off into a reason that makes **YOU** feel you have no deal. I quote the words of many famous losers in the industry,

"THEY ONLY CAME FOR THEIR GIFT"

2. **Do you want another five minutes sleep?**
   You're wasting time already! **WAKE UP**. That five minutes can lead to another ten minutes, you hit that snooze button again and again, lying there in your dream world of being that best Timeshare Sales Professional in the world. Well stay there, because all you are doing is **DREAMING**.

3. **Are you hung over?**
   The answer to this question is "you are your own boss". You are the CEO of your own corporation **Y.O.U. Timeshare inc.** Do you think the CEO or president of a million dollar a year plus company wakes up for work hung over after another night drinking?

   When you meet the drinkers in the Timeshare industry, and there are many of these all over the world, all scraping by, pay day to pay day, living off their stories of when they were top dog, and trying to tell you of all the closes they thought of and the big deals they once did. **BORING.**

Watch them run to the bar straight from work and have to keep leaving resorts as they have another bar tab they cannot pay.

Do you see where this is leading?

This is not the best way to start your day, it's got NO SALES TODAY written all over it......FACT

Put yourself in the position of opportunity.

These first moments of the day are so important. You must set your mind and your attitude ready for whatever life throws at you. It makes you prepared. It is a habit that you will enjoy doing, because when you think about it what is the alternative?

Every day is an opportunity for you. Yes some days you can get up to go to work and your mind is not with it. You may be in a bad mood, the slightest thing can set you off - traffic, the weather, you name it, you roll into work all full of negativity, everything is wrong, of course it's not your fault and then you get a tour.

You do not want this tour. As soon as they give you an objection it's your reason to close your manager saying there is nothing there. This of course leads to the tour finishing pretty quickly, say less than ninety minutes. Then you get another one and do exactly the same. At home, your husband, wife or partner asks *"How was your day? Did you get a deal?"* Your words of course are, *"No chance, nothing there at all, the clients were rubbish, just wanted their gift."* Another day in Timeshare has passed. An opportunity to earn money that went, mostly because of your attitude.

Have you ever had a day like that? Be honest with yourself.

So if you control your attitude and use every day as an opportunity, stay focused, and stay sharp you will get more sales, you will be happy in your work and you will earn more money. Sounds simple doesn't it, and yet we all know that selling Timeshare is not. What I am saying is **put yourself in the position of opportunity every day.**

Right now the question you must be asking is,

"How does the way I wake up affect whether I am going to get a sale today or not?"

This is where I want to introduce you to self talk. Self talk of course is what you say to yourself, this can be out loud or mostly what you say to yourself when you are doing your day – to - day things.

Let me give you examples of typical self talk that we use when we wake up. Most of this is habit; we do not mean it, it's just the way that we talk to ourselves.

"I have not got the energy today"

"Oooh it's cold"

"I wish I could lie in bed all day"

"Wonder what crappy tour I will get today"

"I bet I don't get a tour today"

"I wish I was rich"

"It's raining, not going to be a good day today"

"I hope I get a deal today"

"When am I going to get clients that want to buy?"

"I am sure those clients were lying to me yesterday"

"Why does Gary get all the lucky clients?"

"I need to get 3 sales or I will not be able to pay my rent"

"Think about it, think about it, that's all they say"

☞STOP NOW

I hope you can now understand why as much of 77% of what you tell yourself may be working against you, and I believe that just by starting your Timeshare successful sales day with positive self talk rather than the typical morning mumbling that we all can do means you are putting yourself in the position of opportunity every day.

CHANGE YOUR THOUGHTS, SELL MORE TIMESHARE............FACT

So as soon as you are awake you start your self talk positive and focused.

> " I feel happy, I feel healthy, I feel terrific."
> W Clement Stone

Wake up, jump straight out of bed and start your successful day. Let me share with you a great tip on how to start your day.

I wake up, get out bed, stand up and raise my arms in the air like an athlete who has just won the gold medal and walk to the bathroom self talking.

"I'm a winner I'm a winner I feel happy I feel healthy I feel terrific. I'm a winner FACT."

Wow, every morning these are the first thoughts and words that enter my mind, so you can be pretty sure I am going to have a good day. You may want to do this, it works and makes you feel great, guaranteed every day. **FACT**

Take a note of what self talk you give yourself tomorrow morning, when you wake up, when you get washed and when you get dressed, when you drink your morning coffee or juice. It's amazing the conversation that you have with yourself in your head. Write down what you say and see if it is positive or negative.

Taking a shower and cleaning your teeth is a good ten to twenty minutes of you and you alone self talking to yourself. Some people sing, but 90% of us self talk. When it's a work day most of your self talk is about the day in front of you and what happened yesterday. This can lead you to thinking about yesterday's tour that did not buy, or a cancellation that happened last week, even what's on the TV tonight or what are you going to have for dinner.

A Sales Professional I met, Larry Coats, who has sold millions of dollars of Timeshare sales in his 20 years in the industry told me that when he wakes up first thing in the morning, and in his words:

"I wake up and think, what am I going to sell today? That's the only thing on my mind."

So let's look at the **right** way to start your Timeshare successful sales day.

1. **Wake up and start positive self talk straight away.**
   The beautiful thing about self talk is it's yours. You do not have to use what I say. Create your own. It's fantastic that you can choose all your own self talk that motivates you. It is proven that most of what we say to ourselves is negative. I am asking that in order to put yourself in that position of opportunity every day, focused and sharp ready to sell, this is the way to start......**FACT.**

   What is the alternative to waking up using positive self talk?

2. **Continue your positive self talk while you wash and shower.**
   The power of affirmations and repeating to yourself that you will sell today is the best free gift that everybody has but only 2% use. Look at the great boxer Muhammad Ali. He is world famous for using repeating self talk or affirmations.

"I AM THE GREATEST BOXER OF ALL TIME. I am going to be heavyweight champion of the world." Whenever he was seen on television or interviewed after a fight this is all he would say, and of course as we all know he was. Tell yourself you are a winner, use your self talk with emotion and passion and you will sell more Timeshare.....**FACT**

"If at this stage this does not seem normal to you, and you are not comfortable to do this, that's fine. If you do not want to be in the top 10% at your resort, if you do not want to earn more money then I suggest you pass this book on to someone who does. I believe 100% that this change in focus, in attitude and belief in yourself will get you more sales. Even if you're good you could get better, just one extra sale a month over a year can mean thousands of dollars more commission."

Look at all the superstars in the world of sport, the top golfers, football, ice hockey, athletics, all the top performers in their field. Tiger Woods knows how to play golf, Michael Jordan knows how to play basket ball, Lance Armstrong knows how to ride a bike. The list could go on. It's their attitude, focus and mental approach that puts them above the rest.

You know how to sell Timeshare. Improve your mental approach and you will sell more.

Feed your mind with positive thoughts starting first thing in the morning. It's the best breakfast you can have. Some people may go to the gym to work out to keep fit and in shape. Your positive self talk is your mental workout every morning before you go to work.

Today is your day

"A positive mind finds a way it can be done, a negative mind looks for all the ways it can't be done."

Napoleon Hill

MUSIC

WHAT DOES YOUR MIND LISTEN TO ON YOUR WAY TO WORK?

Now your journey from your home to work is a fantastic opportunity to really control your thoughts. You have started your day off with positive self talk and you are all focused ready for your day ahead. Your journey to work, no matter how long it takes, is your opportunity to motivate your mind and really lift yourself.

"Music is What Feelings Sound Like."
Author unknown

I love music. I really feel that type of music you listen to can put you in the mood you want to be in. Those favorite tracks you have that always get you smiling, as well as the ones that give you memories of great times in your life.

Just try and listen to sad love songs on the way to work for one week and I wonder what sort of a week you would have, and how your mind and attitude would be? It's a fact that uplifting music, fast with beats, can get you going just as well as slow depressing music can bring you down.

Take a moment now and think about your favorite music. I want you to take your time and list about ten songs. These will be ten of your favorite songs of all time, or any uplifting songs that get you going.

Think about great times in your life, your wedding, school memories, that first song that was playing when you met your loved one; that cd that you always play before you go out on a night out, any motivational music.

Take your time and think of your ten favorite songs and write them down. They do not have to been in any particular order, just as they come into your mind.

1

2

3

4

5

6

7

8

9

10

Now you have your ten, I want you to circle your top three. These three songs must be your favorites. Just thinking of them makes you feel good.

With technology today it is pretty simple to get these songs onto a cd or mp3 player. Most people can do it and if you cannot, you know someone who can. What I want you to do though is to make a point that for the next thirty work days you will listen to these three songs every morning on your way to work. **EVERY MORNING.**

Never miss a morning, get into the habit and make sure you listen to them, be it in the car or through headphones as you walk or catch a bus.

By having ten songs you can rotate through the year, always having a different top three, maybe change your top three every thirty days. This will make a great impact on how you arrive at work ready for your tour and your opportunity. Get in the zone, do what professionals do, they focus and shut themselves off. By listening to music on your way to work you are stopping outside influences of negativity entering your mind, for example listening to the news or hearing other negative conversations.

It's your world, your thoughts and now you are listening to music that makes you feel good......**FACT**

My top three are

1. **Rocky theme tune, Gonna Fly Now by Bill Conti.**
   Wow, this one works for me. It does not matter how I feel, this song just lifts me. I AM WINNING. Raise those arms in the air. You are a Champion.

2. **Gabriel's Oboe, by Ennio Morricone. (Theme tune from The Mission)**

I love this tune, it's from the film The Mission, great moving movie and also a tune that I got married to so every time I hear this it makes me feel happy. (You must have a tune that makes you feel like that.)

3. **I Have a Dream, by Abba**

    Listen to the words of this song – it's all about goals, dreams and belief. I quote a line from the song, *"and my destination, makes it worth the while."* How do you know whether you have got there, if you do not know where you are going?

All this time in the car to work I am having a great time feeling good about myself. I pull into to the car park ready, 100% prepared, they could give me a tour as soon as I walk through that door and I would sell it......**FACT**

I feel that confident and I have such a strong belief about myself and remember,

BELIEF DRIVES PASSION

Do you arrive at work ready to walk through the door like that, a strong passion to sell today, do you?

Imagine being like that every day for two months - how many more sales would you achieve? One or two, or how about one a week extra? That could be an extra fifty sales a year: and you have only just arrived to work.

Look at your colleagues and how they arrive, moaning about the weather, traffic, yesterday's tour that did not buy, some are even still going on about last week's tour that did not buy. Are these the top performers at your work place? I very much doubt it, so stay away from them.

"Music is the Medicine of The Mind"
John A Logan

A high percentage of your sales are down to your attitude. You have now raised the game, and raised your focus.

By starting your day with positive self talk and closing your mind from negative things that are happening around you, you will become stronger.

Why would anyone listen to the news in the morning? That happy news story of what is going on in the world. Listening to fifteen minutes of news before work is listening to negative information about wars, missing people, troubles in the world, bad weather - you name it bad news sells, all of this you could be feeding your mind before you take your tour.

Just by listening to the news for only fifteen minutes a day, you are listening to five hours a month of this before you go to work. That's nearly three full days a year.

Replace the sixty hours a year of negativity with sixty hours of motivation.

Replace listening to the news with listening to
your music, your thoughts, it's your day.

For those of you who have a longer journey to work it's a great idea to add a motivation cd as well. There are many great audio cd's which you can obtain, this is just like attending a seminar without having to travel. Imagine sixty hours a year of motivational seminars. That's like attending five or six seminars a year without leaving your car.

I would recommend anything by Napoleon Hill, Dale Carnegie, Earl Nightingale, Norman Vincent Peale, Brian Tracy or Dennis Waitley.

You can find these links to these on www.thetimeshare coach.com

To take it to the next level you could also write out your own self talk script. I have done this myself and found the results amazing. Write a fifteen to twenty minute script of your own self talk and record it to cd or an mp3. This can have a major impact on your thoughts and your feelings.

For example,

I am a winner, I am organized and in control of my life. I am a winner.

I am healthy, energetic, and enthusiastic and I am going for it.

Nothing can stop me now.

I like who I am, I am in tune, on top and in touch.

I have determination, drive and self - belief.

I am living the life I choose, and I chose what's right.

I respect myself and I like who I am.

I have made the decision to win my life and that's what I am doing.

Today is my day. My clients like me and trust me and they know what I have can benefit them and their family.

1 in 4 of all the clients I see join.........FACT

I welcome objections

I never get clients that want to 'think about it'.

Imagine your own script that you play to yourself every morning. Your own morning meeting telling you how great you are and how successful and professional you are at selling Timeshare.

I have seen 12% closers close over 25% in weeks just by using positive self talk and affirmations every morning.

Notice I say every morning, you can not expect this to work by just reading it once or twice and then expecting a dramatic change, but you will see one if you make it a habit and do this every day.

Their pitch did not change, their clients did not change, but their belief and attitude did. The same clients that up fronted them with all the reasons for not joining, became members. WHY? Because the Sales Professional let all the excuses bounce off them, they were winning regardless of what they had in front of them.

That's the difference between the top performers, and those from the middle and the bottom.

ATTITUDE

It is not often you will read in a book so much detail about preparation in the morning before work, normally you would read:

Get up early, dress for success, be prepared and focus.

Yet I wanted to go into more detail as to what your thoughts are from when you awake in the morning to getting to work, and what you feed your mind, and how focused you must be.

Don't wake up and watch the news, how depressing hearing all the time of the bad things that are happening in this world. Why even pick up a newspaper? Feed your mind positive uplifting thoughts of what you are going to achieve that day. It's your day and these first moments can determine what will happen the rest of the day. Put yourself in the best position and above the rest.

This is what the winners do, why not you?

TIMESHARE TIPS
TO REMEMBER
Part One

YOUR FIRST THOUGHTS OF THE DAY

Just as you feed yourself a healthy breakfast and juice first thing in the morning and go for a jog or work out in the gym for that healthy living, feed your mind positive thoughts all the time from when you wake up.

Use self talk and positive affirmations.

> *"I wake up and think what am I going to sell today? That's the only thing on my mind."*
> *Larry Coats*

> *"I feel Happy, I feel Healthy, I feel Terrific."*
> *W Clement Stone*

A negative frame of mind and a positive frame of mind can not operate at the same time. What frame of mind do you choose?

Your Subconscious mind does not know the difference between good or bad, Positive or Negative. It believes anything you tell it with feeling. THAT IS A FACT

Pick music that lifts you - I mean really lifts you and makes you smile, listen to these songs on the way to work. Do this for thirty days and notice the difference in your performance at work.

"You either ride life or it rides you.
Your mental attitude determines who
is the rider and who is the horse."
Napoleon Hill

THE TOUR
PREJUDGING

TO JUDGE BEFOREHAND WITHOUT
POSSESSING ADEQUATE EVIDENCE

Prejudging will lose a Sales Professional many a deal when a sale could have been there... **FACT**

Prejudging is the cardinal sin of all Sales Professionals and everyone has done this at some time in their career.

The skill to master is to never prejudge. You have no right to prejudge your clients. As the dictionary meaning says "to judge beforehand without possessing adequate evidence."

How can you have adequate evidence to decide if the clients you are about to tour will buy or not just by looking at what they wear, or where they are from?

Turn to the front cover of this book and read the under heading,

Change your thoughts, Sell more Timeshare FACT.

You can have all the sales training in the world and learn all the closes, yet your mind can play tricks on you. You may have a great product, a natural skill to warm up your clients and use your takeaways and tie downs but your mental attitude is the key to selling more Timeshare.

NEVER PREJUDGE

This can be one of the most basic comments you will ever hear in your entire Timeshare career. It is not rocket science yet a simple way to not give your 100% best in a presentation.

You can motivate yourself through positive self talk to be focused; sharp ready for your next tour, yet life can throw challenges at you that can affect your mental attitude from being 100% positive.

For example you may,

Have not had a sale for a few days,

Just found out you had a cancellation,

Be speaking with negative people before you go out on tour,

Problems outside work

Many things can cause your mind to not be 100% focused and when this happens it can start to affect your performance when selling Timeshare. This leads to negative self talk, blaming your clients and prejudging.

These are standard prejudging comments that Sales Professionals will say before a tour:

"Oh no why me? Look at the state of them, they won't buy."

"Children!!!! I can never get a deal when the children are running around everywhere."

"From Kansas, I never get a deal with people from Kansas"

"Teachers – great, they always want to 'think about it'"

"Finland? I hope they can speak English - this will be a quick tour"

"On an exchange? Great, they already own, I bet they tell me they have got enough"

"Man without his wife, this has to be a GI"

You could write the rest of this book with all those reasons why we prejudge our clients and assume already that they will not join. It can be as simple as what they wear or where they are from. We think we know.

"Whenever doubt creeps in treat it for what it is; a doubt. Believe your beliefs and doubt your doubts."
Napoleon Hill

The dream is the well dressed couple, with the Rolex watch and flash handbag that look like they have plenty of money - yet many times these people do not join.

A pet hate of mine, and please remember this is only my view, is when a Sales Professional will get their tour sheet and judge straight away that the clients will not join just by looking at where the clients are from.

NEVER DO THIS.

How you can judge whether someone will join or not just by looking at their address is beyond me. Yes, it can be light - hearted but remember what you are feeding your mind. You must feed it positive thoughts.

"A Positive mind finds a way it can be done,
a Negative mind looks for all the
ways it can't be done."

Napoleon Hill

So How do you not prejudge?

Look at every sale as an opportunity to make a sale, not lose a sale. When you get your tour just look at the name, find out where they are sitting and go out there and greet them with the biggest smile you have - projecting positive thoughts to their mind that what you have is perfect for them, they need this and it will benefit them.

This is the key point, you have a couple, there is a 99% chance they take vacations. Yes they want their gift but you have a product that can benefit them and their family. You Must Believe this, Do You?

Prejudging is a word that you must take away
from your vocabulary.

Why bother to prejudge, there is no need and nobody gains from it. The top Sales Professionals will look for the opportunity to sell regardless of where the clients are from, what they wear and how they look. There is always an opportunity to sell......**FACT.**

Another way that many Sales Professionals prejudge is due to the fact that they have superstitions that they cannot sell to people from certain places, or clients that have children on tour, even that they cannot sell Timeshare to clients that already own.

"Superstition is a form of fear; it is also a sign of ignorance. People who succeed keep open minds and are afraid of nothing."

Napoleon Hill

YOU HAVE to treat every client the same no matter where they are from or what they do, every tour. Now it can be difficult in our job to maintain this high standard performance time after time. There will be days when you can get your third or even fourth tour and really just do not like the look of the clients in front of you. If you do exactly the same every tour, no cutting corners, your full a to z presentation but adapting it to each different client, you will see your performance figures - and more importantly your wage packet - rise.

Sounds simple? Maybe not, but it is all about just changing your mindset and not prejudging. This is not one of the hardest things to do as all you need is a bit of coaching, but it is the hardest thing to maintain.

To always not prejudge will take a lot of skill, but again it's a choice and all skills are learnable.

Just want the tour - do not think about where they are from or what they wear or how they look. We all know of the many tours that looked like they could not afford anything yet got out the platinum credit card at the end of the presentation. This has happened and always will.

You have to not let that negative self talk in your head control the rest of your day, or you will lose the sale as soon as you meet your clients.

Clients form very quick judgments. They make up their opinions about you in the first ten seconds, and this affects their entire attitude toward what you have to sell them.

Going to greet your client with your mind already made up that this is not a sale changes your whole image. You can walk out to the client,

"Morning how can I help you?"

"So what do you want?"

No effort, you have just switched off completely. Sometimes these clients have a real interest in your product, perhaps they have been recommended or have had bad vacations before and want to get value for their money. But five minutes of your negative attitude towards them and guess what they are not buying, well not from you anyway.

As far as you are concerned you spin them and then go and tell your manager that there was nothing there and they just wanted their gift. You know you are right is what you say to yourself, as you knew they would not join. If you keep this pattern of thought your closing percentage and pay check will drop, **you have to go the distance no matter what, and never prejudge.**

That is what this book is for, to stop that happening no matter what you have in front of you. You give it 100% every time you do not blame or prejudge your clients at all. You stay focused as it's a numbers game - 1 in 4 join so you must do your full presentation every tour, because you just never know what is going to happen.

First: what is the alternative, to go back and sit in the office with all the negative Sales Professionals that are bottom of the line due to their low closing, or go out and give it your best? You are on commission only, this is your opportunity. It's a much better feeling to know that you have gone the distance and have not missed a sale.

It's better than not trying. Keep digging away, find the hot spot and find out what vacations they take.

I know its OK for me to sit here and write this but I have been there, I have taken these tours. Some will never buy no matter what you do, it's not for everyone. Yet you should still do your full presentation every time.....**FACT.** I am sure you know this too if you have been in the business at least a year.

Do not let your self talk turn negative telling you what is going to happen before you have even started.

So how do we control our self talk?

We use affirmations; we fight the negative self talk as soon as it comes into our thoughts, replacing it with positive self talk.

To stop prejudging I suggest a powerful self talk affirmation that you can use before you go on tour. Please remember when you say this, say it with feeling and passion, it makes such a difference.

"I am a great Sales Professional. When talking to a client, I am guided as to what to say and how to say it, so that I will be successful in gaining their interest in that which I am selling."

Write this down, keep it on you and repeat this before **EVERY TOUR** you take for the next thirty days. You will stop prejudging as your mind will not have chance to. Take control, more positive food for the mind, let's sell Timeshare today.

Go straight out and shake your clients hands with great eye contact.

You must beat that negative self talk away from you. As you have been doing since you woke up this morning, feed your mind with positive thoughts. Take control of your mind, it's your choice: Control your thoughts.

Remember, your thoughts are the only thing you have complete right of control at all times. "Right of Control" means that you *can* control it, it does not mean that you *do* control it. You must learn to exercise this right as a matter of habit.

Now just because you beat that negative self talk away, then please remember it is not going to just leave you and go "OK then". While you are sitting with your tour it's waiting for your clients to say something negative so it can say "told you so", it's waiting for them to say,

"Look we are just here for 90minutes to get our gift."

"We are not signing anything today."

"How long will this last? We have to get away by 12!!!!"

"Is this timeshare - oh we thought it was a hotel!"

Again that negative self talk hits you, telling you that this is a waste of time, let's get rid of these, spin to win, next, there's nothing here at all. You have only been with them five minutes and already you are thinking nothing is there.

At this stage time and time again a high percentage of Sales Professionals give up and let the clients close them. This happens more when you are on a bad run and have not had a sale for a few days.

From waking up, getting to work and going out on tour, you have fought the negative thoughts. You have taken control of your mind, and then afterwards you have decided not to prejudge what you have seen from a distance. You get in front of your client and hear them speak. You would love to hear "we want to buy" but that never happens, instead, you get front end objections.

Please do not give in now, not after all the hard work you have done before you got this far.

You should welcome objections. Objections are the best bit of the tour, this means you have a job to do so agree, confirm and overcome them. Don't be beaten by the first objection you hear, look forward to it.

At the start of this book it mentions how talented Timeshare Sales Professionals are.

This is because they have the hardest job to do, to convert a negative approach into a positive sale. Remember, our clients do not come to buy, they have barriers - your job is to relax them and get them to like you and trust you.

Getting the client to like and trust you is the most important part of the tour because if they don't like you or trust you they will not buy from you.

It has been said that from the first moment you meet your clients they are deciding whether they like you. Books cannot teach someone how to do a meet and greet or teach someone to do a warm up. This is your job; it's up to you, you are on stage, you have to perform.

> *Yet you have the only audience that gets to pay after your performance.*

SO MAKE IT GOOD

Research shows that the money you make in any endeavor is determined only 12.5 percent by knowledge and 87.5 percent by your ability to deal with people.

There is no need to write a chapter on how to warm up your clients. The best tip is for you to be and act yourself. Please do not be false, the clients will spot this straight away and see you as another typical Timeshare salesperson. Be sincere. Just because they like walking or sailing, do not go "wow I love walking and sailing" if you do not. Show an interest of course, find some common ground but be normal not false. You know how to do a warm up, it's like talking to someone in a bar, and it's how you got through the interview when you got your job.

> *It's people skills.*

This is not a book to describe how to do the perfect tour please remember that. Of course you meet and greet your clients and warm them up. That is standard in Timeshare. I want to get to the key points that can stop your belief and may lose you sales leading to negative thoughts. This stage is quite an important part of the tour where you get your first objection. These of course will continue throughout the tour.

So let's assume that you have beaten all the negative self talk in your head and you are focused positive and have made friends with your clients. They like you, and you are building trust. You have set the stage of what's ahead - you do your intent statement and all you ask is for a yes or no at the end of the presentation!

Welcome to front end objections.

OBJECTIONS

OBJECTION, DOUBT, OPPOSITION, PROTEST.

What are objections?

It has been said that they are not a "no I do not want to join" but a "please tell me more as I am not convinced enough yet to say yes." I believe this is a much better way to look at an objection.

All our life we hear objections - yet as a child that does not stop us, so why do we let it as an adult?

> *If you cannot handle objections then*
> *you are in the wrong job.....FACT*

Too many Sales Professionals come into this industry, get a few sales, think it's easy and then spend the rest of their life waiting for people to buy. When they get objections they straight away think there is no sale and try to finish the tour as quickly as possible.

A question to you: there is a new fabulous five star Timeshare resort, being built in a tropical paradise. It's right on the beach, every condo has an ocean view, the price is amazing and it's the only Timeshare resort on the island. The demand for this product is very high.

Now in order to get best performance we are going to form two sales lines,

Sales Line A and Sales Line B

Which line would you like to work on?

Line A only takes the clients that come in to buy.

Line B only takes the clients that come for their gift, will only stay for 90minutes and have no intention of signing in the day.

Which line do you want to work on? Which line will make you more money?

Line A or Line B?

If you choose line A you will go out maybe once a month; if you are really lucky maybe more like twice a year.

If you choose line B you will take 2 tours a day every day and you will close 1 in 4 with the right attitude and belief in yourself and your product.

It is a fact. Your clients only want their gift and only want to stay 90minutes and have all the objections you could think of. **Does that bother a Sales Professional? NO**

They stay focused and work smart; they ask the right questions and get the clients to like them.

They have a positive mental attitude regardless of the weather or what life throws at them.

A Timeshare Sales Professional
Welcomes Objections.

This job is never going to be easy that's why your earnings are unlimited; it's your job to improve yourself and welcome the challenge every day. You have covered the pre tour mindset from leaving home, getting to work to the being in front of your clients and ready to sell to them. You have covered the negative self talk in your mind that is there to put you off selling and replaced this with positive self talk looking for all the opportunities to sell today.

You know you will get objections so you have to stay focused and you continue doing your presentation.

Do not cut any corners and welcome any objections you get. handling them in a professional way.

The best way to handle objections is.

AGREE CONFIRM and OVERCOME,

For example when an objection is thrown to you do not knock it, that will only put the client's back up and even in this early stage of your presentation you can lose your sale. Don't make the client look stupid either, a man does not want to look stupid in front of his wife and vice versa; do not come across as the cocky Timeshare rep that they are expecting. Any objection that is put to you, agree with it.

AGREE WITH ANY OBJECTIONS!!!!!!!

Let's look at the key front end objection that you will get on tour, the world famous,

"Just so you know we will not make a decision today."

This is the classic, you hear all the time.

Please let me share a few tips on this line. (Please remember these are tips. Throughout your Timeshare career, take all the tips you can, learn them memorize them and put them across in your own words, they must sound genuine and from the heart not from a script.)

"That's a fair comment Mr. Jones - I would not expect any of the clients I see to make a decision on anything within five minutes of meeting me. The clients I see only decide to join us because they want to. You have to buy this not be sold this. If you want to join us of course you can purchase today and if you don't want to that's fine by me. But first let's see if our product fits your vacation needs."

Or how about,

"I agree John and Mary yet studies have found the very best time to get someone to make a decision is at the end of the presentation. It's not because it's some crazy manipulative closing technique. It's because as Adults they are going to have more information to make a decision than they are ever going to have in their entire lives.

So if at the end of the presentation with information you have, you find you,

Do not like the accommodation,
We do not have resorts you want to go to,
You do not trust the company,
And it's not affordable for you to join.

What's your decision going to be?

Client "NO"

"Exactly - yet if at the end of the presentation with the information you have you find that,

You do love the accommodation,
We have resorts you want to go to,
You trust our company,
You can comfortably afford to join and of course you want it.

What's your decision going to be?"

Client "*Yes*"

"**Thank you**" (shake hands) and go straight back into warm up.

"**So where do you like to take vacations?**"

These are a couple of ways to respond to an upfront "We will not make a decision today" line from your clients.

Before I started writing this book I said to myself that I did not want to fill the book with loads of closes and answers for you to use as I have always felt in trainings that I have been to and books I have read that they are good for knowledge and you must know them, yet they are no good just reading them back to your client.

They must sound believable and have passion.
They must come from the heart.

The key point is when a client says to you that they will not make a decision today, **don't fight it**. This can happen many times when you do your intent statement or break the pact. You must expect this. With a good warm up a Sales Professional can overcome this, yet if you fight it at this stage then you can lose any chance of a sale already.

"Look John and Mary I will be asking you for a Yes or No today."

Client *"well we will need to think about it"*

"Well I will take that as a no then."

Or the client says they can't make a decision today and the Sales Professional throws it back – "well that's a decision, not making one, isn't it?"

This may be smart but it will not take you closer to getting a deal. So why bother?

Be professional: don't fight it, expect it.

It is a fact, that when a client up fronts you with the statement that they will not make a decision or will not sign anything today, there is a high chance that this is going to be a sale.

Ask all the top performers on your sales line and they will say that they would much prefer to hear a client straight up front saying they will not make a decision today than a client saying "we are interested in this". It is fatal to hear someone say they are really interested straight away. They do not always buy. Ask anyone who has been in the business for a few years how clients that up front you with a "we will not sign today", end up signing, and their first words at the end are,

"Oh I can't believe we are doing this, we promised we would not sign anything today."

That is a fact all over the world.

Don't fight objections welcome them, want them and if there are not any create them.

CREATE OBJECTIONS!!!!!

Without objections you are just leading to a 'think about it' at the end of your presentation. You go through your presentation and all you hear is yes, yes, yes. This causes many new Sales Professionals to the industry to get very excited thinking that the tour is going to be a sale. The clients rush you along agreeing with everything you say, they love it. All they want to know is the price, that's it, **"how much does it cost?"**

Then you quote **"is there anything apart from the money that will stop you joining us today?"** and of course the clients say no.

Then when the price is put down, many reasons for not joining today come out

"We want to think about it" - the most polite way of saying no.

"You did an excellent job"

"We need to speak to our lawyer or accountant"

"Once we finish the house extension"

"We are putting the kids through college"

They won - you lost - learn from this.

Create objections; if they are not giving you any then they will not be buying from you. No one buys a prod-

uct of any sort that costs thousands without asking questions or giving an objection.

> *Yes, you still have to pay your*
> *maintenance fee every year!!!!*

For example when you explain about the maintenance fee wait to see if they ask "does it go up?" This has to be asked. When presenting the maintenance fee and what it includes, you must always wait for the client to ask if it goes up every year, and what stops it doubling. This is a key question to see if your client is interested or not.

A lot of non - buying clients love to use the maintenance fee as a reason for not joining.

"What bothers me is that you have to pay a maintenance fee every year."

Please agree with that line, as we all know that you pay for it when you take other vacations anyway.

If you are a true professional and believe in your product you can cover this all the time.

Maintenance fee is a good thing. Install that in yourself.

A great way to present the maintenance fee is to say,

> *"Your maintenance fee is $$$ and*
> *this is why people join."*

When you present the maintenance fee be proud of it. It's your job to present it, explain what it's for, where it goes and how the quality is guaranteed. You know you can compare it to what they spend on vacations anyway. If you have belief in your product and yourself this will not be a problem.

.CTS

> many Sales Professionals who are low closers use the maintenance fee objection as an excuse and accept it when the clients use it as a reason for not joining.

2) **No owner of this product has a problem with the maintenance fee, only the non - owners.**

With objections, *"we will not sign anything today"* is probably one of the most common front end objections. Look forward to it and welcome and handle it professionally.

At the start of this chapter I said that objections are a **"please tell me more as I am not convinced enough yet to say yes."**

There are of course many others as well, maybe too many to list, and of course too many which do not mean anything at all.

A lot of front end objections do not mean anything, they are just lines to throw you off scent. All clients have an in-built defence mechanism that causes reflex actions. These reflex actions are mostly minor objections which should be completely ignored. A Sales Professional will not even acknowledge minor objections and will continue their presentation as if they have not heard them.

There are though three key questions you would expect from a client on tour, these are:

1) *Will I be able to get what I want?*
2) *Does the maintenance fee go up every year and by how much?*
3) *Can I sell it?*

The reason you want these questions is because they give you a chance to throw negatives into your presentation. Now to many of you this will sound insane but I think it is very important to tell a client the facts, positive and negative. This gives balance to your presentation.

"NO you will not get the exchanges you want all the time. You have to book in advance."

"YES the maintenance does go up every year!"

"YES you can sell this but do not look to make a profit on it, this is not an investment like buying a house, it's an investment in vacations for you and your family."

I have seen many a presentation where the Sales Professional has told the clients everything is so great even to the extent to saying you are guaranteed sunshine!!!

"Can I go to Hawaii?" No problem.

"Can I book late and still get a 5 star resort in Spain in August?" No problem.

"Will I get an ocean view, top floor?" Of course you will.

"Can I sell it?" Yes and you can double your money as well.

This is what gives our industry a bad name, and most of the Sales Professionals selling like this are not around when the clients get back as they have moved on to another resort. Also any clever client will either, think it's too good to be true and not buy, or buy because they are so sold but cancel when they get home, once they have checked things out and find they are not true anyway.

Please remember that your clients are expecting you to tell them how fantastic and amazing your product is. They are on a Timeshare presentation. Timeshare presentations are talked about all over the world. Most of the talk is about "you can never get what you want" and "the maintenance fee goes up every year". So of course your clients are going to ask you questions like this. How you answer them plays a big part on the trust part of your tour.

It is a fact that to get a 5 star resort in Spain in July or August on an exchange. Or to exchange to a ski resort in February or Hawaii in the high season and get the resort you want. You really have to make your request in advance. Hand on heart we all deep down know this.

Unless you own an ocean front Timeshare you have to request an ocean front.

You should love to tell your clients this because it shows you are not afraid to tell them the truth - it builds trust, especially if they buy and get speaking to owners on the resort and the owners back up what you have been saying. The clients will be more likely to proceed with the purchase as you have told them the truth.

Do not lie to your clients, there is
no need to......... FACT.

Be proud to throw negatives in. Do not go over the top but be professional. A big point is when clients ask if they can sell their weeks. You do not want to be telling clients they will lose a lot of money, because of course they can sell their weeks and yes some can be sold at a profit, for example if you are buying pre-construction or at a very high demand resort. But please give it to them straight. A simple rent versus own pitch will always cover this.

Remember it all depends on what you are selling: points, pre-construction, 5 star, fractional, all these products have different value. The main point here is that they are buying and owning a vacation product. Their money is going from their pocket A to their pocket B, it is still their money and there will always be a value at the end. If they rent their vacations it goes out of pocket A, and it is gone.

What we have discussed here are awareness points that I have found, used and also learnt from some of the top closers in the business.

PUT NEGATIVES IN. **It builds up trust** and you need to do this with the 21st century clients that you see today.

We have spoken a bit about objections and how to handle them, and also putting negative parts into your tour. These are sales tips that I hope may assist you. Whatever company you work for will have presentations guide-lines, like your pitch or your funnel. That will never change, that is how it was sold and will always be sold. You as a Sales Professional must stick with this and adapt when need be.

I wanted to continue from negative parts to the common sense part of the tour. You of course have to get your clients to like you, all the way through the presentation, build trust and handle objections. A key point though is: when you ask questions, to involve both the clients.

The experienced people reading this now will think "is this a Timeshare sales book for dummies?" yet so often we can all miss this point. Being a man I would so often get tied up talking to the man in the presentation about soccer, a big love of mine. I knew that I had to bring the woman in and would, but sometimes it would seem false, with her knowing I was just being polite. As I write this I am thinking how this is a standard part of the presentation, yet I am also thinking how much we put it to 100% practice. Only you know the answer for this but it's good to have it here to remind you.

Always involve both. Most of you will find when you do your presentation that it is the man doing most of the talking, yet as we all know it's the woman making the decisions. This can be switched, when the woman is doing most of the talking it's the man that makes most of the decisions. Your job as the Sales Professional is to involve both.

The very simple way to do this is just by turning the answer you get from John or Mary to the other,

"We like to go skiing twice a year" **says John**

"Why is that?" The Sales Professional asks

John gives a standard reply and then the Sales Professional will turn the answer to Mary,

"What do you like about skiing Mary?"

You may find out then that Mary can't stand skiing or that she loves it. What you are doing though is involving both your clients; you must do this every tour.

The highly skilled professional will always involve both clients FACT. The Sales Professional will study in their mind the reactions he or she gets and dig deep to find that hot spot or buying motive.

Another main reason, I believe, is because it is the woman that makes most of the decisions when it comes to vacations. A fact: studies show that,

WOMEN DECIDE 92% OF THE FAMILY'S VACATION

From my experience at work and at home I believe this is true. So please make sure you involve the woman in your presentation. Too many times you can hear:

"he makes all the decisions" and you move on as you have great rapport with the man, yet back end at the table you find it gets passed back and you hear those famous words *"we have to think about it"*

It's not rocket science yet it is a simple tool that can often slip away. **Involve both your clients and ask the right questions.**

YOU HAVE TO ASK THE RIGHT QUESTIONS

We all know the basic things to ask,

Do you take vacations?

Where do you like to go?

What do you spend on vacations every year?

Do you plan to take vacations for the next 10years?

The list could go on, just make sure it is not like an interview. No presentation should sound like that. It has to flow smoothly like talking to your best friend. Plus remember if they have been on presentations before they know what you are asking and why. The art is to ask them like you are genuine, you are interested in what they are saying.

"John & Mary do you mind if I ask you a few questions on the way you take vacations? This way I can present our product so it fits your vacation plans. I do not want to show you our resorts in Hawaii if you do not want to go there?"

This is the skill, asking and then listening. If you want to be good at this job you must learn this skill, and it's again a skill that can be learnt. Remember

ALL SKILLS ARE LEARNABLE

Ask the questions, get the answer and then ask one of the most important words in your sales presentation.

WHY?

ASK WHY, ENGAGE YOUR CLIENTS, IF THE CLIENT SAYS IT THEN IT MUST BE TRUE

Why is such an important word and one that must be remembered. So many times it is easy to shoot off loads of questions to the clients, get all the information you think you need and then present the product, in most cases telling the client why they should buy.

You have found out that they like to go to Florida.

They like to have quality accommodation and would prefer an apartment or condo to booking two hotel rooms. Away you go putting your point across on why they should buy your Timeshare.

Yet your job could be so much easier if you let them explain **why**. Look at this question:

"Do you prefer a hotel room or an apartment or condo?"

"Oh we would prefer an apartment."

"Great, you will love this because as a member you can stay in high quality apartments, condos and even town-houses all over the world."

The above is fine and you may pitch this way, yet let's look at how different the question and answer can be just by adding the word why.

"Do you prefer a hotel room or an apartment or condo?"

"Oh we would prefer an apartment."

"Why?"

"Well we prefer the space and the comfort and kitchen facilities whether we use them or not."

"Great, you will love this because as a member you can stay in high quality apartments, condos and even townhouses all over the world."

Just by adding the question why, you have engaged the client into the real reason and remember: **if the client says it then it must be true.** Now that the client has told you why they like apartments or condos over a hotel room, you can use that throughout your presentation.

I know this is common sense to most people but I have included it here as a reminder so that you always use this.

"Where do you like to go on vacation?"

"We love going to Florida."

"Why do you love going to Florida?"

"Oh there is so much to do and the children love it."

"Are vacations important to you?

"Yes."

"Why is that?"

"It's a great time to be together. No work, nice to relax and have fun times."

"Is accommodation standard important to you?"

"Yes definitely"

"Why?"

"We expect good standards when we holiday and you should always stay in accommodation as good as your home if not better."

As you have read this you must be thinking "what a lay down", and I know these are text book answers - you will not get these replies most of the time, it's not always that easy.

These text book answers are great to ask **why,** and smile in your head as you get all the ammunition you need as you get closer to a sale.

You tend to find that when you ask **"why"** when clients are giving you an objection or negative response to the questions you ask, you will find out how genuine it is. Remember, ask it all the time as it also lets the clients speak more while you listen

To close on this please remember it is a great way to tie the clients down throughout your presentation as you can always resort back to the moment they told you, (When showing resorts) you know you told me you want to go to Florida and location is important to you.

(When in show apartment) you know you told me that the standard of accommodation is important to you.

(When on walking tour) you know you said that you must have activities for children.

(When pricing) earlier you mentioned that $350 a month was comfortable for you.

> *Ask "why" - engage your clients. If*
> *they say it, then it must be true*

ASK FOR THE SALE

You have got to ask for the sale, not just at the end but throughout the presentation. This is a FACT.

While working with some Sales Professionals on improving their closing percentage we discussed about asking for the sale. Many felt uncomfortable doing this, yet if you do not ask for the sale early on then you are leaving everything down to the end.

If you only ask your clients to join at the end of your presentation, where do you go if they give you an objection?

NOWHERE, IT IS TOO LATE

It can be very easy to wait until the end to ask your clients to join. Why rock the boat? When the clients are agreeing with everything you say and asking buying questions and you feel that this is going to be a sale, why ask them now? They are going to say yes at the end.

BIG DANGER SIGN!!!!!

There are many reasons that stop a Sales Professional asking for the sale throughout the presentation; these can be when you are new to the industry or even when you are having a bad run of tour no sales. Confidence can be low in both these cases so asking for the sale early and not getting the answer you want is not the preferred option.

They like it,

They love all the places they can exchange to,

They **yes** you **yes** you with every question you give them and ask you lots of buying questions about how it works. Oooh this is going to be a sale. You put down the price, make it affordable and what do you hear?

> *"You have done a great job but we*
> *want to think about it."*

NO SALE

This is what happens in most cases if you do not ask for the sale throughout your presentation. Create the objections, bring them out and overcome them.

It should always be down to the money.

I believe about half way through the presentation, after you have shown the clients what they are buying and how they can exchange, you must ask them what is going to stop them joining today? **And then shut up and wait for the answer.**

> *Stay quiet and wait for their answer;*
> *do not say it for them.*

Ask your clients this question.

> *"So you have said you like what you have seen so far,*
> *what is going to stop you joining us today?"*

What is the worst thing that is going to happen? The clients will say nothing, or most likely say *"the money"* or give you an objection like *"we do not know if we could use it"* or "I am not sure it works".

If they say nothing, which 99% will not, then stick out your hand and get the paperwork ready. I do not think this has ever happened to me but it has to some people I know, and it may happen to you once or twice in your career.

Most likely they will say *"the money"* or *"we do not know how much it costs"*. That's good and of course the obvious answer to that would be **"so if it's comfortably affordable I am looking at two new members today?"**, or words to that effect. To which the reply is mostly *"well how much does it cost then?"*

Please be careful here and do not blow your whole presentation by teasing your client by saying "I will tell you at the end". Be professional. You do not have to tell him the exact cost, I agree 100% with pricing at the back end but you must put some prices out there.

YOU MUST PRICE CONDITION

"Well John & Mary you can join us for as little as $350 per month, but it all depends on what size of unit, and the season and view that you want to buy. Before we get into how affordable it is to join, I have two more things I want to show you so you can really see the value in becoming a member."

This is just a tip that you can use or re-word to say something that you feel comfortable with.

You are the Sales Professional, you know what to say - take these ideas and adapt them to you and your personality. As I have said before, make it sound genuine and from your heart. The key point we are discussing here is asking for the sale.

When you ask your clients what will stop them joining today and they do not say "the money", you will also get a reason, an objection, and again that's why it is good asking the clients who have been saying **yes yes yes** to you and love it so much, whether they are going to join today, because in situations like this on tour it's time to find out if they are just stroking you or are clients that really want to join

For example you are doing a great presentation, your clients love it and when you ask what would stop them joining today, they come out with *"oh we can not join today as we have an extension going on our house."*

Now at least you have found that out now and not at the back end when it's too late to work on it.

Most of the time you will hear,

"I would love to join but I am losing my job when I get home."

"It sounds great but we have to put the children through college."

"This will be better for us when we retire."

"We never make a decision on the day."

"This is the first one we have looked at."

NO MATTER WHAT THEY SAY AGREE WITH IT

Throughout your career you will hear hundreds of reasons why they are not joining, 90% of the time they are just smoke screens that mean they are not sold yet. By asking for the sale half way through your presentation you get this out, agree with them, confirm them and then overcome them, and move on towards the handshake and the *"yes we want it,"* which converts to cash in your bank.....**FACT**

I hope you understand what I am saying here because a high percent of Sales Professionals do not ask for the sale right until the end of the presentation and when you get objections and excuses then what can you do? You can batter it down while at first you get over the complete shock that they did not tell you before. But did they have to? You should first admit to yourself that you blew it. You should have found that out a long time ago before you even got to the back end so you know what is going on.

Ask for the sale throughout the presentation.

Of course please do not meet your clients say hi and then ask them if they are going to join today. That is common sense and of course do not even ask it in your warm up.

Get you clients excited so that they are asking you the right questions and you can hand ownership over to them. This is when you say "OK you are now an owner what would you do this year with your week, come back to this beautiful 5 star resort or exchange it for somewhere exotic?" Watch that reply because if it is *"I do not know,"* **you need to keep working big time.**

Yet If they are giving you good feedback then always ask them what will stop them joining. Now you are selling, now you know where you are heading, the rest of your presentation is really getting them to want it want it **TODAY.**

NO IS GOOD

For every ten tours that you take it is very rare that you will get a "no thanks we do not want to join". You always get a **think about it, not today** or **great job we will buy from you later.** Most of the time this means not sold; they just are being polite to you.

So when you get a NO, smile and enjoy it. Fantastic, shake their hands and move on. Not everyone is going to buy so make sure it is a **No,** not a **think about it** and get your client to agree that really they are not going to join.

No is good. Please welcome a No. It is very hard to get one but a No should make you feel great. When you get a No that means there is nothing there. All the top Sales Professionals hardly get a **think about it.** You should 100% understand that a **think about it** is only a nice way of saying No. When they say to you "I want to think about it", ask them how long they need.

Most replies will be "oh a couple of days" or "when we get home we will let you know". This is just pathetic. Look back at all your sales that have joined on the day. They wanted it so they joined, anyone who wants to think about it does not want it so do not let them close you into telling you they do want to join but just need more time.

Remember all the negative people at your work the low closers who never get deals because they believe they have done a fantastic tour yet the clients are going to let them know next week.

Well check their pay packets; they do not earn any money because they let the clients close them. On every tour and every sales deck around the world someone closes someone. You close the client, or most likely the client closes you. Accept it as a fact and do your best to make sure it does not happen again.

The top Sales Profesionals in this industry do not hear "we want to think about it"

They hear yes or no, and that is a fact!!!!!!

SHORT TOURS

This is common sense, and the easy way not to get sales. Short tours. How can you get someone to part with thousands of dollars in less then sixty minutes? Some of you may do that, but I guarantee most of the sales will cancel. Short tours play a big part in the difference between top and bottom performers. Short tours show that the Sales Professional has given up. They have heard a few objections and thought **nothing here**. They close their manager and spin them. I wonder how many short tours could become sales if they had just stuck to the tour pattern, done a good warm up, got the clients to like them and done a full presentation. Please note that too long tours can lose you sales, it's no good doing a five hour presentation as most of the time you will only bore your clients, so where is the balance?

As a Sales Professional you decide this. What a simple answer you may think, but every tour is different. Most cases a meet and greet with a warm-up should take at least 30 to 45 minutes. A famous saying is "How long does a warm up take?" **As long as it needs to.**

Many years ago when Timeshare first started you would not even talk about the product or use a survey sheet for ninety minutes minimum. But the industry has changed now and you must adapt. Some clients, a small few, will be difficult to warm up, these can be called drivers. You must take control though. If they do not want any chit chat tell them that you need to ask them a few questions about the way they take vacations so you can adapt your presentation to suit them. Then you do your warm up while you ask them the questions.

TAKE CONTROL, MAKE THEM EARN THEIR GIFT

All you need to do is get the clients speaking about what they like to do and show a genuine interest in them.

A great question is not to ask what they do for work but say **"does your job affect the way you plan your vacations?"** This will introduce you to what they do. Again show a real interest and do not just ask the man and then forget the woman: remember, make sure you involve both.

Some of you reading this will say but they do not always want to speak to you like this.

Well they are not warmed up then.
Make a friend make a sale!

Ask them to talk about their vacations, where they went last and why, what they enjoyed - and listen with a real interest. Some tours it might not happen, so get them out of the seats if you can and walk them around. If you have a sales deck or credibility wall, and of course a walking tour and a resort to show them, use it. **DO NOT** do that every tour, only if your clients are proving difficult to get excited, but often it will work - then bring them back and start on your presentation; all this though can help you extend your tour time and make you feel you went the distance.

This is the key point, going the distance every time. Any short tour will show that you must have spent less than twenty minutes on your warm up and twenty minutes on the presentation. You should be able to spend at least thirty minutes on an rci or interval brochure. Do not overdo it showing them every page of the book, but use common sense.

All your successful sales have been ninety minutes to three hour tours. My advice is a two to three hour tour will put you in the position of opportunity.

A one hour warm up including your discovery, finding out how they take vacations.

A one hour presentation, plus a one hour walking tour including back end pricing. Don't do it by stop watch but this is how the successful people stay at the top. They do long tours and never cut corners. It may be hard sometimes when you feel you have nothing in front of you but this is why you have the opportunity to earn more money than most of the couples in front of you put together.

The Tour and your success from your tours is the difference between a good long successful and wealthy Timeshare career and a very short unhappy expensive one. Prejudging, objections, negative parts of the tour, why, asking for the sale and short tours are all key points that you can re-learn and use from time to time to relight your presentation.

The tour of course is your bit, your selling skills. It's why you are the best of the best.

Everyone does their tour differently. There are many other key points from painting pictures, warm up, walking tour if you have one, financial logic, 3rd party stories - all of these are important parts. I would expect of course you would have been taught these when you joined the industry and are of course learning more all the time. It is your job to make sure you are sharp. These are standard parts of your presentation and every Sales Professional will use them in different ways.

Let's move on to the clients that we see on tour, as I feel it is important to look at what is in front of you. Not in a prejudging way but to get wise to the clients of the 21st century.

"A smiling face often defeats the cruelest of antagonists, for it is hard to argue with the man who smiles when he speaks."
Napoleon Hill

CLIENTS OF the
21st CENTURY

The way Timeshare has been sold has changed dramatically over the years, and this is mainly due to the changes that have come to our industry. You have to adapt your presentations to the clients that you see in the 21st century. They still expect the hard pressure old style presentation which makes their pact even stronger. Many have been on presentations before or definitely know of people that have. There are also many challenges which can make your work more difficult.

Rescission period, cooling off time, 7 days or 14 days

Resale companies

Internet

Neighbors over the garden fence (*"what, you bought a Timeshare?"*)

The image of the Timeshare presentation

Rescission period, cooling off time, 7 days or 14 days

There used to be a day when you would be pitching a client who had just got out of a taxi, sent to your resort on the promise of receiving 200 cigarettes and a t shirt, if they attended a 90 minute presentation. You took the client on a tour with a pitch pad and a brochure, showed them a video, told them anything that they wanted to hear, got their credit card, rang the bell, picked up a spiff the next morning and were paid all your commission two weeks later.

So much heat was pitched then,

"Your maintenance fee stays the same for the first five years."

"A 1 bed exchange can get you a 3 bed."

"It does not matter when you book your week, you always get what you want because you own gold crown."

"As owners you only pay half price for all flights."

This list would write a book itself. It is not good or clever, anyone can sell that way, you do not have to be trained at all and it gave the industry a bad name - hence many people who own timeshares that have been sold that way are not good ambassadors for it.

A lot of owners found out a year later they could not get the exchanges that they wanted and the maintenance fee had gone up!!!!!!!.

So laws have come into place to protect the client and I feel this is a good thing, and you the Sales Professional can use this to your advantage.

Notice the word Sales Professional as that's what you are now, In the old days you were a closer, a pure sales machine, yet with the clients of the 21st century that you see today, they can spot a close a mile off, The Sales Professional closes without the client noticing. **AND THAT IS A SKILL.**

You should be pleased to have the rescission period there. Be proud of the product you sell and what it does, you do not have to lie and you do have to tell the facts. Sell the product the way it works. Whatever product you sell, points or weeks, sell it as it is.

If you have to book 12 months in advance tell them. If the maintenance fees go up every year tell them, because just the slightest conflict from what you have told them to the clients finding out differently can lose you a sale.

Sell Timeshare as it is but also - and this is a big tip - once you have sold to your clients you are only half way there. You must work them through that rescission period.

The rescission period is there to give your clients the confidence to buy without pressure, and your job now is not just a 90 minute pitch selling your Timeshare just to grab the money. It's a sales presentation backed up by a full follow-up in the form of a call 2 days from the clients getting home, a postcard sent to them, even send flowers, all the simplest things to keep your deal in bed. Build a relationship with your client that gets you more sales in the future and plenty of owner referrals that buy from you as well.

All you have to do is present the facts of what your product does. **THERE IS NO NEED FOR HEAT OR LITTLE WHITE LIES.**

Do not be scared of the cooling off period or rescission; it is there, so use it to your advantage. The only Sales people who do not like this are the pitchers who just bang deals down and hope they stick. NO NEED

The rescission period is a great tool, yes you work a little bit harder yet a Sales Professional can work a little bit smarter.

I know of a Sales Professional, one of the best in the industry, who sends a hand written note to the clients thanking them for joining and they get flowers sent to their home as well. Also when the clients leave dreaming of that dream holiday they are going to have on their first usage, he sends them all the details they need about the country they are going to visit from the tourist board. Wow, no wonder his cancellation rate is non-existent. And this is a proven fact that even with the rescission period you can still sell and still sell more, as it gives the client peace of mind when entering the purchase.

AND THIS SALES PROFESSIONAL WRITES OVER $3 MILLION OF TIMESHARE EVERY YEAR.

Many Sales Professionals just sign them up and that's it. They just wait for the funds to come through. Selling like this can lead to many of the sales cancelling, buyers remorse, no follow up, the lot. You must not do this if you want to get paid. It's the other half of the job, yet so easy to forget.

Remember, you have sold it - they are in, now all you have to do is just back up what you said and help them plan their vacations. Call them, send them flowers, these small efforts can come back to you time and time again.

First: because they continue to pay up and complete their purchase.

Second: because they then send you referrals as well.

This is simple business sense and what any CEO of a company will do.

Think of the rescission period as a good thing, it is there and it's never going to go away ....**FACT.**

Use it to your advantage. You should want your client to go home and have it checked out by their lawyer or whoever gives them peace of mind. What they are telling you is that they want to join, and if everything is what you have told them then they are members. When a client says that, it's music to your ears because you know your product checks out and you know you have given them the facts.

MAKE A FRIEND, MAKE A SALE, DO YOUR FOLLOW UP, KEEP THE SALE.......FACT

Resale companies & The Internet

The Internet can be your friend or your enemy. Just type the word Timeshare into any search engine and look what you find.

SELL YOUR TIMESHARE NOW.

TIMESHARE RESALES.

CHEAPEST TIMESHARES IN THE WORLD.com

And of course everyone's favourite THE TIMESHARE ADVISORY GROUPS. They make me laugh, a group of people who can advise you on what to buy and how to buy it!!! They probably work for the resale companies anyway.

Resales are in every product for sale in the world. Timeshare resales are there, so you must pre-empt this on your presentation. Never shy away from it, 99.9% of your clients will do research when they get home, and with freedom of speech available on the web so much can be written about Timeshares.

Your benefit is that the relationship you are building with your client will make them loyal to you.

As Jeffrey Gitomer says and – he has written a fantastic book on this quote,

Customer Satisfaction Is Worthless, Customer Loyalty Is Priceless

Plant the seeds that resales are out there. Some people will disagree, and say that you should not bring this up at all and that is fine, it's your choice. I feel, though, that if you do not cover it the clients will see it anyway in daily newspapers or on the internet.

Sell service, full company backup, sell third party stories on why your other clients bought from you. Buying cheap can always work out expensive, ask any top performer in your company, they do not have a problem with resales, it's the low performers that do.

It is another reason to blame, an excuse as to why their sale kicked, when really they did not cover this or do a good follow up.

The internet is there to your advantage, use it. You can show clients how easy it can be to book, a one stop travel shop is just at the click of a button. So many non-owners book online now, so this is just changing the website they use, but now they book as an owner not a tenant.

You will find many forums with happy Timeshare owners sharing advice on tips on exchanging and great resorts they have visited. The internet is the future, it's how the clients of the 21st century book their vacations and get their information. It's how the world communicates now. So you must welcome it.......**FACT**

Neighbors over the garden fence *("what, you bought a Timeshare?")* & The image of the Timeshare presentation

The Timeshare industry is booming, FACT. Annual sales run into the billions world wide every year, and double figure growth for the past ten years. We now also have brand names like Marriott, Hyatt, Disney, Starwood, Sheraton, Four Seasons and many more that have seen the benefits of this great product.

I think as the years grow the image of a Timeshare presentation is improving. It is down to us to keep it that way. If you told someone that you sold Timeshare, they used to think you worked on the streets of Cancun with a scratch card putting people in Taxis. Those days are long gone now, and with more and more people buying Timeshares every day around the world soon the neighbors over the garden fence will be saying:

> *"We own a Timeshare it's fantastic, you must go and see our sales person, they delivered everything they promised."*

The big positive is that there are thousands of couples all over the world buying Timeshare every day, and even

with all the obstacles that can be there they still go ahead and purchase and then enjoy fantastic vacations world wide. You have to adapt to the clients of the 21st century and be clever how you sell.

TIMESHARE TIPS
TO REMEMBER
Part Two

TIMESHARE TIPS FOR YOUR TOUR

How can you have adequate evidence to decide whether the clients you are about to tour will buy or not just by looking at what they wear, or where they are from?

Look at every tour as an opportunity to *make* a sale, not *lose* a sale. When you get your tour just look at the name find out where they are sitting and go out there and greet them with the biggest smile you have projecting positive thoughts to their minds that what you have is perfect for them, they need this and it will benefit them.

Superstition is a form of fear; it is also a sign of ignorance. People who succeed keep open minds and are afraid of nothing.

Do not let your self talk turn negative, telling you what is going to happen before you have even started.

I am a great Sales Professional. When talking to a client I am guided as to what to say and how to say it, so that

I will be successful in gaining their interest in that which I am selling. Repeat this with passion and enthusiasm every time before you go on tour.

Remember, your thoughts are the only thing of which you have complete right of control at all times. "Right of Control" means that you *can* control it, it does not mean that you *do* control it. You must learn to exercise this right as a matter of habit.

You have the only audience that gets to pay *after* your performance, so make it good.

Welcome objections they are the best bit of the tour and if you do not get them you will never get a sale, you are being stroked. Also through negatives into your tour. This is so important. It builds trust and shows you are not the typical sales person who only tells them how great it is........ FACT.

If you can not handle objections then you are in the wrong job. . ...FACT
A Timeshare Sales Professional welcomes objections.

Put negatives in, it builds up trust.

It is a fact, your clients only want their gift and only want to stay 90minutes and have all the objections you could think of. Does that bother a Sales Professional? NO

Ask the right questions and ask them like you care. Do not treat your warm up like an interrogation or an interview. Make a friend and get them to like you. Listen with empathy and remember to ask Why, engage your clients; if the client says it then it must be true.

You have got to ask for the sale, not just at the end but throughout the presentation. This is a FACT.

A No is good

The top Sales Professionals in this industry do not hear "we want to think about it"

They hear *yes* or *no* and that is a FACT.

Take control, make them earn their gift.

Make a friend, make a sale.

The clients of the 21st century can spot a close a mile off. The Sales Professional closes without the client noticing. AND THAT IS A SKILL

There is no need for heat or little white lies.

Use the rescission period to your advantage.

The internet is the future, welcome it.

Adapt to the clients of the 21st century and be clever how you sell.

> *"Destiny is not a matter of chance, it is a*
> *matter of choice. It is not a thing to be*
> *waited for. It is a thing to be achieved."*
> *Napoleon Hill*

PMA, PERSONAL DEVLOPMENT

POSITIVE MENTAL ATTITUDE

Selling Timeshare is like a mental rollercoaster, as many things happen that can take your mind up and then down.

Hold a positive mental attitude at all times. You will read that in every personal development book, of course - how you can sell if you are not in a positive frame of mind?

Having a positive attitude day in day out is not an easy thing to do.

No tours, cancellations, not the pay check you expected, going for weeks without selling and of course as we have discussed getting a client that wants to think about it.

All these things happen overtime, and how you deal with them is your choice. That's why at the start of the book it says that you choose the thoughts that you have in your head and you choose how you react to situations that happen. You have to realize that some things are not in your control and the more that you think about these things and waste energy on them, the more it is stopping you from performing at your best when you are next on tour and also when you get home to your family.

A classic line used in this industry is NEXT and that's what you should do, move on.

Focus on the now not the then.

You will find at every resort in Timeshare, Sales Professionals and these can be usually some who have not been in the business that long who just love talking about non-buying tours. They also share great interest in your non buying tour. OK a very small number do care, but most just ask all the time how your tour went.

Why do they ask this? Because this can lead them to telling you about their tour that did not buy, and they will go into so much detail, they love it.

Please stay away from:

NEGATIVE PEOPLE AT WORK

Negative people just drain you of all the energy that you have and if you are not careful you will fall into the same trap. There isn't any point in talking about non-buying clients at all, unless it is in a positive way for you to improve. Yet negative people talk about their non-buying tours like it is a soap opera. Whenever you hear them going on about their non-buying tours that have got on the **be back** bus, listen carefully to what they say as they never blame themselves, to them they have always done a good job.

"I asked all the right questions I did everything that I was trained to do."

Well guess what? You didn't. You did not sell them at all. They sold you.

Remember, there is a sale at every table. The clients close you or you close them, someone is closing.

It is a shame but negative people are part of the work place. They are everywhere, and to be fair some of them do not know they are being negative, it's just the way there are. They like to gossip, they want to know about everything and everyone, yet do not take much effort in self improving their work performance. They get the odd deal and get by. I love the saying **even a blind squirrel can find nuts** and have heard that many times from people who see the unexpected when certain sales people would get deals. Yet the negative people are such a drain on you. They let go of their negative energy and pass it on to someone who is willing to listen. It can be a bad tour or the fact that they are not getting any tours, a deal may have cancelled or the weather may be grey, they just are not positive......... **FACT.**

> *"The only real time is NOW. It is crucial to remember this. Any time spent thinking about the past with guilt or regret is wasted time. All you can do with the past is learn from it."*
> Napoleon Hill

Wait for your next morning huddle when updates are being given to you. That same person will put their hands up and go for the negative quote just because they like being heard. They should form a union and work in a large factory, yet here they are at your Timeshare resort. They claim to come to work for the money, yet give themselves so many obstacles to stop them from selling. I could write pages on these people but I will not Why? Well what's the point, it's a waste of energy and time. That's what I feel about negative people, **Why what's the point?**

Look at now, right this second and do not blame anyone. Stay away from these people. Again look at the winners where you work, look at the leaders, **in this job it's today not yesterday: it's today, it's now.**

So be positive, get excited about it because as Napoleon Hill said **"through every adversity comes the seed of equivalent or even great benefit"** - this meaning how you react to the setbacks that can come to you every day.

How you react to situations

How you react to situations is your choice and this plays a massive part in your success in the work place and even at home. I want to concentrate on the work place as in Timeshare you have many situations thrown at you every day.

It's part of the job that you might not get a tour until after lunch, how do you react to that?

You might feel that all the clients that you get do not suit your product, don't qualify or do not take vacations. How do you react to that?

You do not get a sale for 2 weeks. How do you react to that?

You have 4 cancellations on the trot. How do you react to that?

How do you react to these situations? Your self talk plays a big part in how you react when things do not seem to go your way.

If you can go with the feeling that through every adversity there comes the seed of equivalent or greater benefit then you will never go wrong. That may sound so simple to you reading this book and of course there will be some situations that can cause you to react straight away in a negative point of view, but always look for the positive in every situation. If you crumbled at every bad situation that was thrown your way then you will not be in the timeshare business within the next twelve months, and that is why for every ten people that start in the industry only 1 will remain 12 months later, sometimes less.

**You have to look for the benefit all
the time, it will increase your energy
and make you a better Sales Professional.**

"I did not get out on tour today" or "it's not fair I did not get a tour today, everyone went out before me"

YOU CAN MAKE THESE SAYINGS INTO POSITIVE STATEMENTS.....FACT

The positive on this would be......

"OK I need to sell my next tour and work my way up the line, everyone is before me because they have sold more than me. I am going to use the time when I am not on tour to learn and get my presentation right. I will look and listen to the top Sales Professionals to see what they do. If I don't get out tomorrow, so what, that's a whole day of extra training for me, but when I do get out I am going to sell - FACT."

"I do not care if they have not had a vacation for years I am going to get them excited and sell to them."

What would be the point of going on about not getting out, and sitting about moaning, you are not doing anyone any favors. Use this as positive down time to make sure you are up the top of the line. You do not see the top Sales Professionals not getting tours do you?

"All my clients do not qualify, they are no good, and none of them take vacations"

This comment only comes from losers, who blame everything in the world but themselves. No Sales Professional would use this line so NEXT move on.

"I have not had a sale for 2 weeks" OK why not?

Take the positive from this, you have not had a sale so look at all the reasons. Do not blame the clients at all. If you blame the clients all the time then how can you improve? So many weak Sales Professionals will not admit they did not do their job. You should always admit to yourself if you did not warm up them up enough or you did a short walking tour.

I once worked with a Sales Professional who had won all the awards you could on line, yet this year he had started low and was not selling.. At the back end of last year it felt like everyone he was touring was joining, and when the New Year started he was so confident in himself, his attitude was like: "Give me a tour - anyone, they will buy."

Yet he was not getting any sales and if they did they were cancelling. We sat down and discussed the differences from last year to now, and this top Sales Professional looked at his tour pattern and had to admit that he was not doing any warm-up at all and he was asking the clients to join in a short space of time, with just a few lines about how great the product was. The good thing was that he spotted it, he went completely back to basics, last year was history it's now that was important and you have to do an A to Z presentation just as it always has been done. If you have not had a sale for weeks take the positive from that, find the reason YOU were going wrong and fix it. Do not be ashamed to ask someone to come on tour with you.

You can not see the picture if you are in the frame!

"My last 4 sales have cancelled"

Take the positive from this, through every adversity there comes the seed of equivalent or greater benefit, and this is so true if your sales have cancelled. Again it's down to you to look for the pattern. Did you tell them they could cancel? Did you sell it or did you just bang it down for a spiff. Did you follow up or did you leave them to get home on their own hoping they would pay their balance?

How about even being pleased if you knew they were good deals but through no fault of your own they just wobbled or got buyers' remorse. Some sales, no matter how good a job you did, will go. But take a positive from it, if it can not be saved then think "Great, my cancellations are gone now for the year let's get on with more sales."

The best way to replace a cancellation is to get a new sale straight away and a good one too. Next month no one cares about the cancellation (apart from the negative people who still moan). Look at it this way: the money was never in your bank so you did not have it in the first place. Keep your pipeline full, the more you write the more will kick but do not write wallpaper, it's no good to you or the team - it's false. You know if you're writing weak sales just to get your name on the board and get a clap in the morning, but soon it will catch up with you, i.e. no money on pay day.

How to motivate yourself when the going gets tough.

So how do you motivate yourself when the going gets tough, apart from finding the seed of equal or greater benefit in all adversity?

Here are some to tips.

TALK TO POSITIVE TEAM MATES. Yes talk to positive team mates you know the ones. They are always happy and selling and always look for the positive in every situation. Also look for the happy people in your work place, they do not have to be sales people. Go and talk to them; it does not have to be about work but talk to positive people, they can always lift you. These should include your partner or a close friend. They do not want to hear about all the bad things at work but they can switch your mind to other, positive things.

WHAT'S THE ALTERNATIVE? This is such a main point, what is the alternative? OK you have had no sales for a few weeks, what are you going to do - Quit? Give Up? If you have read personal development books before, you have always heard about Thomas Edison who invented the light bulb: it took him 10,000 attempts, yet did he give up? Of course not, and that's the thing with bad runs at work - we all have them but what's the alternative, quit? I read a quote which really moved me, by Lance Armstrong the great cyclist who won the Tour de France seven times after battling back from cancer. He says he would have never won any Tour de France if he hadn't got cancer. Why? Because when he was diagnosed, it taught him that pain is temporary, quitting is forever. Please remember that line as it is so true. **PAIN IS TEMPORARY. QUITTING IS FOREVER.**

"A Man is never a failure until he accepts defeat as permanent and quits trying."
Napoleon Hill

VISUALIZE SUCCESS. Whenever you feel low or are having a bad time, find somewhere quiet where you can relax and be on your own and visualize yourself having success. See yourself achieving what you want, see yourself getting those 3 deals on the trot, picking up that big pay check. Your mind is so powerful and one of the great things is being able to daydream. To daydream whatever you want. So visualize in your mind success, success comes in CANs not CAN'Ts. Remember that and see yourself being a success. You have to let your mind know you can do it.

"Imagination distinguishes winners from losers."
Napoleon Hill

TAKE A BREAK. If you are having a tough time or a bad run just switch off for a day or two. Use your days off not to dwell on the past and what has happened but to enjoy yourself. A manager of mine always used to say if I was not performing to my best, go out tonight and enjoy yourself; let your hair down, just be in tomorrow on time and get me a deal. Switching your mind on to fun and away from the pressure you put on yourself can really help you. You're not looking all the time for that client that just comes in to buy. You just do your job and enjoy yourself. This is a very important point here as clients can spot a Sales Professional who has no confidence, and usually when they throw a front end objection and you have not had a deal for a few days and think *oh no not again why me* this will show through.

Switch off, enjoy yourself, have some fun. This leads to another tip on how to motivate yourself when the going gets tough, and that is to **focus on everything that is good in your life.**

You're alive, live it that way.

Look at all the good things you have; your family, your health, you can see, walk, touch and of course you can talk. Dennis Waitley was asked how to motivate yourself when you feel you have problems. He said go to the local hospital and visit the burns unit, or visit the children's ward. Then you will realize you do not have any problems at all.

You see when the going gets tough that's a good thing. It's your job to work that bit harder. You are on commission only, and earn what you are worth. Do not blame the clients or the resort or anything. Do not wish it was easier, wish you were better. Smile and be happy and look forward to every challenge that comes your way.

GROWTH

Struggle is good! I want to Fly!

Once a little boy was playing outdoors and found a fascinating caterpillar. He carefully picked it up and took it home to show his mother. He asked his mother if he could keep it and she said he could if he would take good care of it.

The little boy got a large jar from his mother and put plants to eat, and a stick to climb on, in the jar. Every day he watched the caterpillar and brought it new plants to eat.

One day the caterpillar climbed up the stick and started acting strangely. The boy worriedly called his mother who came and understood that the caterpillar was creating a cocoon. The mother explained to the boy how the caterpillar was going through a metamorphosis and becoming a butterfly.

The little boy was thrilled to hear about the changes his caterpillar would go through. He watched every day, waiting for the butterfly to emerge. One day it happened, a small hole appeared in the cocoon and the butterfly started to struggle to come out.

At first the boy was excited, but soon he became concerned. The butterfly was struggling so hard to get out! It looked like it couldn't break free! It looked desperate! It looked like it was making no progress!

The boy was so concerned he decided to help. He went to get scissors and he snipped the cocoon to make the hole bigger and the butterfly emerged!

As the butterfly came out the boy was surprised. It had a swollen body and small, shrivelled wings. He continued to watch the butterfly expecting that, at any moment, the wings would dry out, enlarge and expand to support the swollen body. He knew that in time the body would shrink and the butterfly's wings would expand.

But neither happened!

The butterfly spent the rest of its life crawling around with a swollen body and shrivelled wings.

It was never able to fly...

As the boy tried to figure out what had gone wrong his mother took him to talk to a scientist from a local college. He learned that the butterfly was SUPPOSED to struggle. In fact, the butterfly's struggle to push its way through the tiny opening of the cocoon pushes the fluid out of its body and into its wings. Without the struggle, the butterfly would never, ever fly.

The boy's good intentions hurt the butterfly.

As you go through your career in Timeshare sales and life, keep in mind that struggling is an important part of any growth experience. In fact, it is the struggle that causes you to develop your ability to fly.

"Through every adversity and defeat there is the seed of equivalent or even greater benefit."
Napoleon Hill

What does this mean; it means that through every tour that is not a sale or every cancellation that you receive or anything that in your mind is not going right for you there is a positive. That may seem strange to yourself at first but if you can adapt this mental attitude towards setbacks or what you may class as failures you can learn from it and move forward.

That is what I love about our job selling Timeshare. You show me a job where you have to fail 75% of your work week to succeed. As much as you may try you will not get a sale every day of your career. Yet if you can treat every *no* that you get as a step closer towards a *yes* then you will succeed. Learn to love *no*'s - please do not get down on them. Learn from every tour, what could you have done to get them closer to a sale.

I was coaching a Sales Professional who was struggling and not selling. She told me that every tour she did was a perfect presentation yet the clients where not joining. The Sales Professional was 100% certain that every tour she went the distance always doing the A to Z, yet she was closing at 13%. To me it is quite obvious that she was not doing a perfect presentation as her closing was too low.

You can not see the picture when you are in the frame yet when you feel that you are doing nothing wrong how can you improve? Admitting that you have under performed, and not gone the distance, is half way there to fixing it, and you need to accept that there could be something in your presentation: i.e not a good warm-up or no closing at all. Maybe just talking, talking, talking and not letting the client speak at all. How can you improve?

Yes some clients will not buy for whatever reason, but if you go at least 10 tours without getting a sale then take a look at the pattern of the reason. If you do not get a sale, look at what you could have done better, not who was to blame.

Blame is a word you should take out of your vocabulary. There is no point blaming your tours or the weather or anything you can find as to the reason why you did not sell or why you are going through a bad run. All of us at times may struggle but read what the story of the boy and butterfly says and find that it is struggle that makes you stronger.

"Remember, a kite flies against the wind, not with it."
Napoleon Hill

If you have had a couple of days of no sales then use this experience to make you stronger. Through every adversity or defeat there is the seed of equivalent or greater benefit....**FACT**. Remember Lance Armstrong said that pain is temporary, quitting is forever - and that is a fact.

Pain is temporary. A *no* sell can very soon be replaced by a *yes* sell.

Get your mind straight and go out and get a deal. Take the positives; if you had a cancellation ask yourself did you really do a good follow up, or were you a bit worried in case they kicked on the phone to you? Did you bang a deal down just to get a spiff?

All the answers to these questions only you know, but it's your business so do not kid yourself. Make yourself strong from this, improve go out get another sale and do a better follow up, make the sale stronger, earn the right to ask for the money. Soon setbacks are out of your mind because you are too busy working out your commission on your next pay check as your have so many sales closing for the next pay day.

Another Timeshare tip regarding struggle and your performance in general is to take time out to improve your pitch or product knowledge. So many people do not do this yet if you want to get better and earn more money then why not? First of all I would like to congratulate you on reading this book as it shows you have taken a commitment to improve your sales performance and earn yourself more money. But before this book, how much time did you spend on improving your pitch, your product knowledge and your personal development?

How many books have you read on sales training and personal development in the past year?

When was the last time you looked at your written presentation? Do you have one?

Personal development and motivation is like nutrition. It must be taken daily and in healthy doses to keep it going.

It has been said that most of us once we have acquired a skill and become proficient in the basics of it usually choose to stop learning, and of course from that point forward cease to improve. This is true of some Sales Professionals. and without a doubt most of the people that come out of the start up sales training who get a sale think it is well easy, and then go weeks without getting any more sales. This then leads to them not getting tours as the experienced Sales Professionals go out before them. Of course this leads to the blame word being used and having no money due to the fact that they are getting no tours and the ones they are getting are not good.

"They do not want to buy. They only want their gift!!!!"

Since this is true of most people it shows the fact that it is only the small minority of people in Timeshare who will go on to become the acknowledged experts. These are the Sales Professional's that receive the lion's share of the income at your work place.

When you look at these facts consider your position at the moment and ask yourself the following questions.

"How good am I at doing it?"

"How much better could I be?"

Realize that if you would study in the field of Timeshare, sales skills and personal development for one hour per day, in one year you would have studied for **15,** twenty-four - hour days. WOW

If you split that into 9 - hour work days that's **Six working weeks** a year of reading or full concentrated studying.

This by just putting aside one hour a day.

Also since you would be only studying for one hour at any given time, you would be able to give the material your undivided attention. Although this amounts to only one hour of study per day, if you were to follow this schedule rigorously, in a relatively short span of time you would stand among your fellow colleagues with so much more self confidence and self esteem that you could not fail.

What do you study in Timeshare? Everything you can.

Learn your interval or rci brochure back to front. Tell me right now a resort in every country in the world that your clients could exchange to. If you do not know then take the time to study. Your clients love to see a confident Sales Professional who knows his product; that gives them more confidence in buying from you. Learn about your resort, practise your presentation. Every year see if you can improve it. Learn more features and benefits. Not only re - read this book but re - read this book every month, even better a chapter a day so all the valuable information can sink into your mind. I have a list of recommendations for you to read at the back of this book. This book and others will give you the motivational food for your brain to take you to the next level in your career.

Tiger Woods with all his skill and money still works on his game as he believes he can be better. That attitude in a Timeshare Sales Professional would be unstoppable.

The test for you though is to make this a habit. It's your choice, you cannot be made to do this. As you read this now, and many other times in this book, it has to come from within. I hope though when you see the cash rewards in your bank, i.e. your pay checks going up every month it might make you more determined to do this. Please let me share with you that since I have followed the principles I am sharing with you in this book my earnings have increased by 60%....... **FACT.** I read for at least 1 hour a day, it makes me stronger and I know my work performance will only get better.

For some strange reason most of us when we leave school seem to stop learning. When you come into the Timeshare industry it is standard to have a 1 or 2 week intense training course and learn your product, but I have seen many people seem to stop after that. OK you have your training notes but for some reason new hires, they get low, do not get sales and seem to start blaming. Do not let this happen to you. Make it a habit to re - read this chapter once every day for a whole month. Take in the information I am giving you. I would also recommend to read the chapter on persistence in Napoleon Hill's book Think and Grow Rich. When you have desire and mix that with persistence you have an irresistible pair. I would recommend reading that chapter first thing in the morning every day for 30 days until it sinks into your mind.

Already you can get started in your study time but do you want to? And do you have the Persistence?

Persistence is a state of mind, so it can be cultivated. With persistence will come success.

You must believe this. If you want something so much that even when you come to the stage where you do struggle, when you have not had a sale for a few weeks, you have had that dreaded cancellation, just keep on going.

Pain is temporary, but if you quit then that is final. When you have persistence you never look at setbacks as defeat, they are just temporary and with them will come the seed of equivalent or greater benefit.......**FACT**.

Belief

Belief, A state or habit of mind in which trust of confidence is placed in some person or thing.

Belief, The feeling of certainty that something exists or is true.

Belief, A strong opinion, conviction.

How good are you at selling Timeshare?

Your first answer to that question is so important.

Sales Professional A says "I am good at my job"

Sales Professional B says "I am OK"

Sales Professional C says "I GIVE IT MY BEST EVERY TOUR. I AM A WINNER, I AM A CHAMPION. GIVE ME CLIENTS THAT TAKE VACATIONS, I DON'T CARE HOW AND I WILL SELL 1 IN 4.......**FACT**.

I believe Sales Professional C will be the number 1 at this resort.

Now to some people speaking that way is like having a big ego or being big headed. Yet what is wrong with that? When you speak like that it is showing that you have confidence in yourself and you believe that you can do it.

Let's say that if you went to the hospital for an operation, would you go with the doctor that said he was good at his job or the one that said he was the best?

If you had a court case to battle out, would you go with the lawyer that said he was OK or the one that said he gives it his best every case and is a winner......**FACT**.

The doctor and the lawyer are not being big headed by saying they are the best, they just have confidence in themselves and their ability to do their jobs.

Having that confidence and belief plays a very big part in your success in Timeshare sales.

What Sales Professional C says is not something you go about shouting around the sales deck and in all the meetings you attend. That would be being big headed and then everyone would want you to fail. This again is self talk.

Say it to yourself as often as you can, **I am a winner, I am a winner**, say it with passion, and when you say it feel it in you that you know it is true. Say it 100 times a day in your head or out loud when you are driving your car or walking to work.

We discussed in wake up about your self talk in the morning, when you take a shower or are cleaning your teeth. What else is there to think about? Take times like this, routines you do every day and feed into your mind positive thoughts. **I am a winner, I am a winner.** You will be amazed at how your confidence levels improve.

How does this happen?

This is because you are giving instructions to the most faithful servant you will ever have, your subconscious mind.

Your subconscious mind will follow any instructions if properly given. It does not know the difference between what is right or wrong, it will act on anything that is fed to it. The subconscious mind responds instinctively to whatever suggestion given to it in an emotionalized state. Hence the power of affirmations or positive self talk.

Instruct your mind with the belief that you will succeed and that 1 in 4 clients that you see join, and you will. That may sound too easy, this chapter shows you how - with a formula of having a definite major purpose or goal that you 100% believe and know you can achieve.

> *"Whatever your mind can conceive and
> believe your mind can achieve."*
> Napoleon Hill

When you use self talk or instruct your mind with positive thoughts you have to say it with passion. This plays a big part in your mind accepting it as true. It is no good just saying once first thing in the morning when you get out of bed, "I am a winner" and wait for the results. You have to tell yourself this all the time morning, night and in the day until your mind accepts this as true. Of course when you say it you have to believe to yourself that it is true as well. You could not say that you can walk on water as an affirmation as we all know that is impossible, so when you use an affirmation know yourself that it is true.

That is why I love the affirmation that 1 in 4 buy. This is always backed up with the word FACT. The word FACT is very powerful. You will notice the use of the word FACT a lot in this book as it cements in your mind that it is true what you are saying. When you say 1 in 4 buy, FACT, you know this is true 100% percent. A wise guy may try saying every client he see buys, yet deep in his mind he would know he would be lying to himself.

What are affirmations?

Affirmations are statements of acceptance that one uses to allow manifestation of your destiny. They are powerful and positive thoughts and statements sent out to your subconscious mind. To do positive affirmations, you need to eliminate the negativity around you. You must first believe that you CAN manifest your destiny. It must be a positive, powerful belief not just "maybe I will try and see if this works".

Together with Visualizations you can create the life you want.

Here is a repeat of a great affirmation to read before you go on tour, **"I am a Fantastic Sales Professional, a Winner. When talking to my clients I am guided as to what to say and how to say it, so that I will be successful in gaining their interest in that which I am selling. 1 in 4 of the clients I see buy.........FACT"**

This is a fantastic affirmation to read just before you take your tour. Read that before every tour for 1 month and watch your performance rise.

If you know you can sell 1 in 3 then say that but you must 100% know you can do it.

Write this affirmation down on a card somewhere and read it. Read it with passion, read it as it is true. As you are reading this now I bet that voice in your head is going *I bet it does not work all the time*. Well kick it out now. You must believe this will work, read the affirmation a 100 times or more and watch your sales performance go up not down.

Timeshare task for you to do.

For the next 30 work days 5 times a day read the affirmation **I am a fantastic Sales Professional.**

Have it written on a card and kept on you at all times. Then find a quiet spot where you can relax and not be disturbed. Go out to the car park, a quiet area on the resort where you work, anywhere, there will always be one. In this quiet spot relax your body, still your mind the best you can and repeat the statement slowly, quietly and with feeling from five to ten times. Do this first thing in the morning at home, three times during the day and last thing at night.

"I am a Fantastic Sales Professional, a Winner. When talking to my clients I am guided as to what to say and how to say it, so that I will be successful in gaining their interest in that which I am selling. 1 in 4 of the clients I see buy......FACT."

When you do this you are feeding your mind more positive thoughts.

Personal development and motivation is like nutrition. It must be taken daily and in healthy doses to keep it going.

Your mind wants as many positive thoughts that it can receive, so feed it with them and watch the wonderful results that happen. The magic power, as some may call it, that we are talking about is not in this book, but it is in you. It's in you and in the application of the principles I am showing you here. We all have it but only some of us use it. All it takes is positive action. (You must though act and not say you are going to act.)

When I have explained this in seminars to Sales Professionals I always spot the ones that do not care about this and hear afterwards from them *what a load of old jumbo*. It's strange that 99% of the time these are the average mediocre Sales Professionals.

To those who understand the mind and how it works, the reason why this principle is so sound is perfectly obvious. The subconscious mind follows the pattern established by the conscious mind.

If a Sales Professional holds a picture of themselves as being average or poor and believes that they cannot do it, the subconscious mind will direct them in thought and action to make them average. Their presentation will be slow and faulty, not sharp at all and when they hear objections they will slowly give up. They will lack the forcefulness to properly impress their clients.

If they see themselves as a fantastic Sales Professional, they will be guided in the thoughts they will express. An enthusiasm will be built up which will reflect in their voice and manner, this will impress the clients. Take the word enthusiasm and take the last 4 letters enthus **I A S M** this can read as:

I AM SOLD MYSELF. This principle is not only effective in the profession of selling Timeshare but in every department of life.

> *"It is very difficult for a man or woman to excel in any endeavor when there is no enthusiasm."*
> *Napoleon Hill*

The best Sales Professionals are the best because they see themselves as the best. The average are average because they see themselves as average, and the poor ones are only poor, because guess what, they see themselves as poor.

I have tested this on Sales Professionals who have been under performing - to tell themselves all day in their head for a week while at work and at home "I am a fantastic Sales Professional, I am a winner" - yet some would say *how can I say this when my figures do not show this?*

Why are you not a fantastic Sales Professional?
Because you see yourself as average.
Change your view now.
Believe you can do it.
You are what you think you are: FACT.

> *"As a man thinketh in is heart so is he."*
> *James Allen*

Thinking

"If you think you are beaten, you are,
If you think you dare not, you don't,
If you like to win, but you think you can't,
It is almost certain you won't.

"If you think you'll lose, you're lost,
For out in the world we find,
Success begins with a fellow's will-
It's all in the state of mind.

"If you think your are outclassed, you are,
You've got to think high to rise,
You've got to be sure of yourself before
You can ever win a prize.

"Life's battles don't always go
To the stronger or faster man,

**But soon or late the man who wins
Is the man WHO THINKS HE CAN!"**

W.D. Wintle

That poem sums up the whole facts. If you do not think you are going to get a deal, guess what: you won't. If you do not think you can be the best Sales Professional on your sales line, you won't. Please remember, all the top Sales Professionals started at the bottom. So why can't you reach the top? You can if you think you can. You can if you believe you can

There are lot of quotes from Napoleon Hill in this book. This is because he has written the most successful book of all time on self improvement, belief, and how to identify your goals. The book is called Think and Grow Rich, and within the book it shows you a secret formula to obtain whatever you want in life and master true and lasting success.

I have read this book many times and the formula in it has changed my life. If you read it, it will change yours too.

The key point in Napoleon Hill's book Think and Grow Rich is the way it shows you the power of having a definite major purpose in life. There is a special way to writing down your goals and how to achieve them. I am sure we all know how to write goals but this formula or that special secret is so unique and it really utilizes the powerful forces of your subconscious mind.

The start of this great book is all about a secret that has made fortunes for more than 500 exceedingly wealthy people whom Napoleon had carefully analyzed over a long period of years. Napoleon Hill was asked by Andrew Carnegie, who at the time was the richest man in the world, to research and organize the world's first philosophy of individual achievement. What made people born with nothing go on to accumulate vast fortunes? What was their secret? Napoleon interviewed many people, the likes of

Henry Ford
William Wrigley
Wilbur Wright
King Gillette
Alexander Graham Bell
John D. Rockefeller
Thomas A. Edison
F.W. Woolworth

These and many more had amassed their fortunes all from a simple formula that Napoleon shares in the book.

The goal of this chapter is how to apply the secret into your work in Timeshare as a Sales Professional. You have got to have a goal, a Definiteness of Purpose, backed up by persistence and a burning desire for what you want.

That's the thing, as 98% of people do not know where they are going, do you?

Where will you be 5 years from now?

Most of us have ideas, plans, that just stay in our head. Think and Grow Rich shows you how to take a desire and make it a reality.

What you want to know is how can you make more sales, improve your closing and earn more money.

> *"Successful people move on their own initiative, but they know where they are going before they start."*
> *Napoleon Hill*

Desire is the starting point of all achievement, the first step toward riches.

You must have a target or goal at work, for example let's say you want to sell 102 weeks in a year or $2 million dollars. Everyone will have different targets, $5 million of sales, 25% net closing at the end of the year, to earn more money than the year before. It all depends what product you sell and really what your own personal goal is. This is the beauty of this, it's your choice what you want to achieve, but it has to be a **burning desire, an obsession.**

It is no good just saying you are going to write $1 million this year, everyone can say that, but with 3 months to go when you are only on $500,000 what do you do then? You are way off your target and it's too late to turn it around.

There are six simple steps that if you follow through with enthusiasm, a positive attitude and 100% belief that you CAN do it -

YOU WILL ACHIEVE YOUR GOALS.......FACT

1. Fix in your mind an exact picture of what you desire

It is no good just saying you want to be the number 1 this year, you need a figure.

If you sell points how many do you need to sell to make you number 1 at you resort?

If you sell weeks how many do you need to sell to make you number 1?

Even better, how much volume do you need to sell to give you the commission that you need to pay all the bills, a bit of savings and the lifestyle that you want?

This work goal, your definite major purpose, is what you want to achieve in your Timeshare work. You can use this method for personal goals in life and family but for the benefit of this book, your definite major purpose is your work goal.

This is where you must get enthusiastic about this. How can anyone on commission only, not want to earn enough money to give themselves and their family the lifestyle that they want, and be willing to do whatever it takes to achieve this?

Ask 99.9% of the people that work in Timeshare why they do this job and they will say *to earn money*. So why don't they earn it then, as only 20% of the people you ask are earning it? The rest get by, deal to deal pay day to pay day, when all they have to do is take control, stop blaming everything but them selves and earn what they want.

Selling Timeshare means you can earn unlimited money. So work out what you need to write in sales to earn the money you need to give you the life you want.

This will not work unless this is 100% what you want. 100% a burning desire, please make it an obsession - not a life one but a work one. You want this so much and you will not stop at anything to get it. Can you do that? It has to come from within.

Many Sales Professionals I have shared this with want it but not enough, it's not burning inside them. Of course we all want to earn 6 figures a year but what are you willing to give in return for that? That is the next step, the step that everyone, when setting goals, forgets.

2. Determine exactly what you intend to give in return for the thing you desire. There is no such reality as something for nothing.

This is what most people do not do when setting goals. It's no good just saying "I am going to write a million dollars this year" and expect to do this, just like that. You must state what you are going to give in return to write that million dollars. This plays such an important part of setting your definite major purpose. Determine exactly what you intend to give in return for the thing you desire, your goal for the year. For example:

"I am going to write 2 million dollars this year. In return for this I will always do a full presentation, no short cuts. I will never prejudge my clients, I will always pitch high and drop when I need to. I will never blame my clients. I will spend at least half an hour a day going through my presentation so I know it will be crisp and sharp and my clients will have confidence in me and what I am selling."

This list could go on and on but I hope you get the point. Everything has a price tag on it.

You must be willing to read the price tag and pay it in full if you are to achieve the target you want that year.

This is so true in life itself. Look at how many people week after week live their life all down to 5 minutes on a Saturday night when the lottery is drawn, that excitement as they expect it's them to who will win the millions they so much deserve. Then in a flash it's over and they spend the rest of the evening looking at how close they were.

"If only it was number 37 not 38, number 2 not 1 and number 23 not 41, then we would have won." I would not like to spend that evening in the presence of that person going on about how close they were.

If you want to make a million dollars then find 10,000 people and get them to spend $100 with you. You can achieve what you want, if you really want it.

Success

If you want a thing bad enough
To go out and fight for it,
Work day and night for it,
Give up your time and your peace and sleep for it.
If only desire of it
Makes you quite mad enough
Never to tire of it,
Makes you hold all other things tawdry and cheap for it.
If life seems all empty and useless without it
And all that you scheme and you dream is about it,
If gladly you'll sweat for it,
Fret for it
Plan for it,

Lose all your terror of God or man for it,
If you'll simply go after that thing that you want,
With all your capacity,
Strength and sagacity,
Faith, hope and confidence, stern pertinacity,
If neither cold poverty, famished and gaunt,
Nor sickness not pain
Of body or brain
Can turn you away from the thing that you want,
If dogged and grim you besiege and beset it,
You'll get it!

Berton Braley

*"Whatever your mind can conceive
and believe your mind can achieve."*
Napoleon Hill

Once you have set your target of what you want to achieve as your goal and decided what you will give in return of it you must then:

3. Establish a definite date by which you intend to achieve this target.

This is where you can adapt this formula to Timeshare. Everyone will have different year start and ends, and also you may want to use this with short term goals. You can even set it just month by month. If your target is to get your closing percentage higher or to reach a certain sales volume you must set a date by when you wish to achieve this.

GOALS ARE DREAMS WITH DEADLINES SO GIVE YOUR SELF A DEADLINE. How can you assess how good you are performing unless you have a set time by when you wish to achieve your goal? This again to most people will be quite obvious when setting goals. Everyone at the start of the year says *"this year I am going to write 2 million dollars"* or *"I am going to sell 200 weeks by Dec 31st."* Simple yes but 98% never achieve it. To establish a definite date by which you intend to achieve your goal is common sense when setting goals, but what most people do not do is:

4. Create a definite plan for carrying out your desire, your goal, and start now!

You will notice there that I wrote desire and then I wrote goal. Desire is the starting point of all achievement. I want you to make your goal your desire your obsession at work the one thing that you want to achieve, no matter what. That is so much stronger than just having a goal. Get excited about it. Unlock the energy inside you. If you expect to create any drive within yourself you have to get excited. To me that is the difference between just setting a goal every year or having a real desire inside you and getting excited about what you want to achieve.

> *"Through some strange and powerful principle of mental chemistry, nature wraps up in the impulse of a strong desire that something which recognizes no such word as impossible and accepts no such reality as failure."*
>
> *Napoleon Hill*

So many Sales Professionals set goals but never achieve them. This is mainly because they just set them, do not have any real desire and do not have any plan to achieve them. **You must have a plan.** It's no good just expecting it to happen. You know how many tours you will have; you know when you have booked a vacation, you know what your product costs and the average sales price, so work out a plan. If you want to sell a million dollars and your average cost price is $20,000 then you need to write 50 deals. Over a year with vacations taken, that's 1 deal a week. This is not supposed to read like goal setting for dummies, but to re- enforce a simple habit that can take you one step closer to earning more money. Whatever your goal is, create a plan.

If your closing is below 10% then you need to make it higher and fast. So create a plan to achieve this. If you need to earn a bit more each month as you want that new car or clothes then create a plan and then do this. This will change your life.

5. Write out a clear, concise statement of your definite major purpose and sign it and date it.

Write down what you want to achieve, your desire.

Write down what you plan to give in return to achieve this.

Write down your plan and time frame and then sign it and date it. This is your contract with yourself.

This simple step is so powerful. **So Powerful.** It works, it really works......**FACT**

It has been said when you put your goals in writing you are 1000% more likely to achieve them.

Yet so many Sales Professionals do not. They never bother.

"It's ok it's in my head",

"There is no need to write it down I know what I want to achieve."

All I ask at this stage in this book is for you to commit to do this for 2 months. I promise you will get more sales, not less. Your closing will go up not down. All this will happen just by writing down a clear concise statement of your definite major purpose, your work goal. Get it down and sign and date it. Then finally, probably the hardest habit to maintain but the final piece of this success formula to help you achieve more sales not less is to:

6. Read your written statement aloud twice daily. Once after arising in the morning and once just before retiring at night.

As you read, see and feel and believe yourself achieving your definite major purpose.

Please stop and just think with your thoughts for one moment on what you have just read in the last few paragraphs. Please just review this before you continue to read.

The reason for stopping is because if you are not willing to do this then I hope you enjoy this book and may I wish you all the best in your career in the Timeshare industry. There are many great Sales Professionals in the world today who do not need to follow these steps and many that will always sell.

You may feel that you are a very good Timeshare Sales Professional, yet by reading this book you must want to get better. Everyone must want to earn more money, to be the number 1 at your resort.

Unless you close at 100% week in week out there is always room for improvement.

Writing down your plan is not hard, probably the hardest part is reading your written statement aloud twice daily. You have to read it first thing in the morning and last thing at night. Every day without fail, every day make it a habit.

A great tip is to get into a pattern. First thing in the morning before you shower or get dressed. Even when you turn the key in your car. These are things you do every morning so use these repetitive times to always read your statement, every morning without fail.

It must became a habit every morning and then last thing at night before you turn out the lights.

When you read, read with passion because you want to achieve your desire so much. Make sure it is the last thing you tell yourself every night before you go to sleep, and then first thing in the morning before you go to work.

> "Hope, Enthusiasm and Faith are key words
> because of their close relationship. When they
> are combined with a definite major purpose,
> they give one access to unlimited power."
> *Napoleon Hill*

Do not just read this like an electric bill or a newspaper. Read it with passion. As you read see and feel yourself already in possession of this.

How do you do this? You visualize.

You need to create a mental picture in your mind of you achieving your goal.

How do I do that? - some of you may ask. It is very easy.

If I say to you the word *steak*. Your mind will create a mental picture of a nice well cooked steak or even one in a butcher's not cooked, you can always create a mental picture.

So picture yourself hitting your sales target, collecting that big pay day and taking your loved one out for a meal;. your colleagues applauding you in the morning huddle as you are Sales Professional of the month. Play it over and over again all the time so your mind accepts this as true, have the faith. Faith is the state of mind that may be induced or created by affirmation or repeated instructions to the subconscious mind by conscious auto suggestion. By summoning over and over again a mental image of yourself already having accomplished your main desire, you will muster the faith you need. Faith is vital to accomplishment. You must have faith that you can accomplish your desire.

That is why you have to set realistic goals that you know deep inside that you can achieve. It's no good being all smart and saying "OK if this formula always works I want to write 1 million a month so this year I am going to write 12 million." Do you really think you can do that? Do you know deep inside that you can, because if you do not then of course it is never going to work. Set high goals but be realistic.

You must not just read your statement like a letter. As you read it see and feel yourself already achieving your desire and then through repeated suggestion, the subconscious mind can be put to work for you. It's the faculty of being able to concentrate your mind on your burning desire until your subconscious mind accepts it as fact and begins to devise ways of bringing it about.

I would like to write pages and pages on how important it is that it has to be a burning desire, yet I can only tell you how important it is. It has to come from within, it has to come form you. As I said before, when you ask a Timeshare Sales Professional why they do this job they will always say *for the money*. 99.9% come to work for the money, yet only the top 20% make it a burning desire, they really, really want it. You must want it so bad deep inside of you, so I ask you: if by following these steps that I have shown means you can achieve your goals and start earning more money, then why not do it?

> *Yoda: No! No different! Only different in your mind. You must unlearn what you have learned.*
> *Luke: (focusing quietly) All right, I'll give it a try.*
> *Yoda: No! try not. Do. Or do not. There is no try.*
> From The Empire Strikes Back, G Lucas

Do or do not, it's your choice.

You should always strive to get better, you cannot stand still you can only go forwards or backwards. There is a saying *you are only as good as your last sale*. Some may say that is negative and you should be positive and say you are only as good as your next sale. That is a choice, to me it's a great motivator as you are only as good as your last sale, what you wrote last year is gone – it's history, you have already spent your commission so move forward, get better and get another deal.

I want to now show an example of what your definite major purpose statement could look like. Please remember this is an example, you must make yours personal. This should give you a rough idea:

My Definite Major Purpose is to sell $................. by the 29th November 2008.

I have sold $ .... by this date and achieved my double bonus for the year 2008.

In return for this:

I go the distance every tour so I know I have earned the right to ask for the money.

I welcome objections and keep working to find the hot spot, and welcome new members to the resort I work at.

I do not prejudge or blame my clients.

If they take vacations then Timeshare WILL benefit them, and if this is affordable then they WILL join.

My time plan is to sell

September . . . . I have sold $ . . . . in 20 working days

October . . . . I have sold $ . . . . in 20 working days

November . . . . I have sold $ . . . . in 20 working days

THIS HAS HAPPENED. NOTHING HAS STOPPED ME ACHIEVEING MY MAJOR GOAL THIS YEAR AS I HAVE A BURNING DESIRE TO ACHIEVE THIS. I WANTED THIS SO MUCH AND I USED ALL MY ENTHUSIAM, POSITIVE ATTITUDE AND BELIEF TO GET THIS. I HAD COMPLETE FAITH THAT I WOULD ACHIEVE THIS GOAL.

WHATEVER THE MIND CAN CONCEIVE AND BELIEVE THE MIND CAN ACHIEVE.

THE TIMESHARE COACH NOV 29TH 2008
$ .... SOLD - FACT.

SIGN
SEPTEMBER 1ST 2008

That is an example, you can fill in whatever amount you choose or you can make it to reach a certain closing percentage. You will notice that the definite purpose set was for only 3 months. That is the beauty of this, it's your goal, your desire so you can set these for 3 months a year or whatever you choose.

Some of you may think it's just a new way of setting goals, maybe it is. But this formula has been used by some of the most successful people that the world has ever seen and you can adapt this to suit your goals in your work place.

As you set out your plan, your statement, remember to include the key points.

What you want to achieve, your burning desire and a date by when you intend to achieve this. Say you want to sell $2 million. The main reason is also that you may get a big bonus. Remember money is what you go to work for. Then move on to present tense, You have sold $2 million by this date and achieved your double bonus for the year 2008. Keep telling your mind that statement twice a day every day with passion and see yourself doing this, and enjoy that nice big bonus to spend on your family at Christmas.

Then you move on to add **what you will give in return for this**. This is important, there is no such thing as something for nothing. Also these are key points for you, reminders that you kept in your head every day. You will go the distance every tour. You must do this, even if it looks as if there is nothing there keep going, do not cut corners, do the same presentation every time - you never know, put yourself in the position of opportunity. Earn the right to ask for the money. How many times have you had sales at the end when you thought there was nothing there?

You then add that: You welcome objections, and keep working to find the hot spot. This is common sense and again a good reminder that you should welcome objections not think they are a straight no.

You do not prejudge or blame your clients. This will help you so much and you will never blame your clients, make this a habit. You will achieve nothing by blaming your clients and as for prejudging we have spoken about this before in the book.

These are the things that you must be willing to give in return to achieve your definite major purpose. Do not just write things down because you think you have to. State what you are 100% willing to give in return for this.

You will know what you are willing to give in return to achieve your desire, and you will be reminded if you are not doing it. **That is why you read your statement first thing in the morning and last thing at night.**

Then **set your time plan,** make it a realistic time plan that you know you can achieve. Please do not be stupid like you are going to get a deal every day, You have never done that before and do not know of anyone who has.

Please use net figures, not gross, anyone can get deals all the time just by writing wallpaper. The professionals know how to keep them in bed. Make your time plan realistic.

Your final statement is a power statement by you which re enforces how this is your burning desire. Please write your own that suits your personality.

Then of course **sign and date it.** Again very, very important. All the above is of no good unless you sign it and date it. As I have said before the hardest bit for you will be to read it twice daily, but if someone came to you and said *read this bit of a4 paper first thing in the morning and last thing at night and you will hit all the goals you desire this year and receive a nice big bonus* who wouldn't? It's up to you.

Remember these are the six steps.

1. Fix in your mind an exact picture of what you desire
2. Determine exactly what you intend to give in return for the thing you desire. There is no such reality as something for nothing.
3. Establish a definite date by which you intend to achieve this target.
4. Create a definite plan for carrying out your desire, your goal, and start now!
5. Write out a clear, concise statement of your definite major purpose and sign it and date it.
6. Read your written statement aloud twice daily. Once after arising in the morning and once just before retiring at night.

ACT NOW, YOUR PERSONAL COACH

Now is up to you. It's your choice. I hope you can take the tips I have given you in this book and put action to them to create more sales and earn more money.

It can sound so simple, you read a book with great ideas on how to sell more Timeshare and improve your closing and earn more money. Yet if that was the case, over the next few months Timeshare sales would double all over the world, the industry would be taken by storm.

This is also true in the personal development field. There are books written all the time with the magic secret that will change your life. Over $500 million worth of self help books and materials were purchased in the US alone last year. Yet only so few take what they read and learn and put it into practice, WHY?

WHY?

I believe it is your habits. You read a motivational book, you get lifted and on a high but after a few days your normal day – to - day life takes over and very easily you slip back in to the habits that you had before. Even the best ideas work only for a little time. You need that constant attention, effort and motivation to stay at the top.

I use the example of working out in the gym. When you stop, your muscle and body can lose the figure and this is the same with your mind. You need to feed it all the time.

Just reading this book is no value to you.
The value is when you take what you
read and put it into action.

I heard a great example that compared positive thinking to golf. With golf you get a good shot and think you have mastered the game, but the next thing you know you fluff your shot again. Like golf, **with positive thinking you have to work at it again and again.**

Look at Tiger Woods, as I write this he is the world's number one golfer yet he will still go out and hit a thousand golf balls a week to work on his swing. If you want to be the number one Timeshare Sales Professional at your resort and get the biggest pay checks then maybe you want to learn more to earn more.

I have yet to find a self development book or training manual that jumps down off the shelf and taps you on the shoulder each morning to say *hi there, do you remember when you read me, and all the positive ideas you learnt that you were going to put into practice, well why are you not still doing them?*

So I ask you to let me be your coach. The Timeshare Coach ^{SM} is your own personal coach to assist you in your daily Sales of Timeshare.

The Timeshare Coach ^{SM} is your strongest believer. He will show you the best in yourself and help you achieve more sales. The Timeshare Coach ^{SM} will give you direction put purpose in your stride, strengthen your will and give you unquestioned belief. He is your own personal coach.

I promise you that if you take all the ideas in this book and put them into action you will get more sales, not less. GUARANTEED.

So this does not become a book you read once but six months later forget everything that you leant, go to www.thetimesharecoach.com

Register on this website along with thousands of other Timeshare Sales Professionals around the world and attend our weekly timeshare sales huddle in the form of an ezine.

You will receive an email newsletter every week with Timeshare tips, motivational quotes and success stories from fellow Timeshare Sales Professionals who have taken the tips they have learnt from this book, put them into action and seen the amazing results.

None of us Are Smarter Then all of us...........FACT

TIMESHARE TIPS
TO REMEMBER
Part three

CONCEIVE, BELIEVE AND ACHIEVE

Focus on the *now* not *then*

Stay away from negative people at work.

Remember, there is a sale at every table. The clients close you or you close them, someone is closing.

Pain is temporary, quitting is forever.

Personal development and motivation is like nutrition. It must be taken daily and in healthy doses to keep it going.

Persistence is a state of mind, so it can be cultivated. With persistence will come success.

Having confidence and belief plays a very big part in your success in Timeshare sales.

I am a Fantastic Sales Professional, a Winner.

You are what you think you are..........FACT.

Selling Timeshare means you can earn unlimited money. So work out what you need to write in sales to earn the money you need to give you the life you want.

You must be willing to read the price tag and pay for it in full if you are to achieve the target you want that year.

Unless you close at 100% week in, week out there is always room for improvement.

Remember these are the six steps.

1. Fix in your mind an exact picture of what you desire.
2. Determine exactly what you intend to give in return for the thing you desire. There is no such reality as something for nothing.
3. Establish a definite date by which you intend to achieve this target.
4. Create a definite plan for carrying out your desire, your goal, and start now!
5. Write out a clear, concise statement of your definite major purpose and sign it and date it.
6. Read your written statement aloud twice daily. Once after arising in the morning and once just before retiring at night.

With positive thinking you have to work at it again and again.

Please find some chapters from a book called As A Man Thinketh, by James Allen. Written over 100 years ago it still rates as one of the best books ever on you and your thoughts. If you are to change your thoughts and sell more timeshare this book is a great tool to read.

As A Man Thinketh is, quite simply, a set of philosophical reflections on the power of our thoughts … James Allen writes: "All that a man achieves and all that he fails to achieve is the direct result of his own thoughts."

Register on www.thetimesharecoach.com and the full version is free for you to download.

AS A MAN THINKETH

INTRODUCTION

This little volume (the result of meditation and experience) is not intended as an exhaustive treatise on the much-written-upon subject of the power of thought. It is suggestive rather than explanatory, its object being to stimulate men and women to the discovery and perception of the truth that—

"They themselves are makers of themselves"

by virtue of the thoughts which they choose and encourage; that mind is the master-weaver, both of the inner garment of character and the outer garment of circumstance, and that, as they may have hitherto woven in ignorance and pain they may now weave in enlightenment and happiness.

James Allen

THOUGHT AND CHARACTER

The aphorism, "As a man thinketh in his heart so is he," not only embraces the whole of a man's being, but is so comprehensive as to reach out to every condition and circumstance of his life. A man is literally what he thinks, his character being his complete sum of all his thoughts.

As the plant springs from, and could not be without, the seed, so every act of man springs from the hidden seeds of thought, and could not have appeared without them. This applies equally to those acts called "spontaneous" and "unpremeditated" as to those which are deliberately executed.

Act is the blossom of thought, and joy and suffering are its fruit; thus does a man garner in the sweet and bitter fruitage of his own husbandry.

Man is a growth by law, and not a creation by artifice, and cause and effect are as absolute and undeviating in the hidden realm of thought as in the world of visible and material things. A noble and God-like character is not a thing of favor or chance, but is the natural result of continued effort in right thinking, the effect of long-cherished association with God-like thoughts. An ignoble and bestial character, by the same process, is the result of the continued harboring of groveling thoughts.

Man is made or unmade by himself. In the armory of thought he forges the weapons by which he destroys himself. He also fashions the tools with which he builds for himself heavenly mansions of joy and strength and peace. By the right choice and true application of thought, man ascends to the divine perfection. By the abuse and wrong application of thought he descends below the level of the beast. Between these two extremes are all the grades of character, and man is their maker and master.

Of all the beautiful truths pertaining to the soul which have been restored and brought to light in this age, none is more gladdening or fruitful of divine promise and confidence than this—that man is the master of thought, the molder of character, and the maker and shaper of condition, environment, and destiny.

As a being of power, intelligence, and love, and the lord of his own thoughts, man holds key to every situation, and contains within himself that transforming and regenerative agency by which he may make himself what he wills.

Man is always the master, even in his weakest and most abandoned state. But in his weakness and degradation he is foolish master who misgoverns his "household." When he begins to reflect upon his condition and search diligently for the law upon which his being is established, he then becomes the wise master, directing his energies with intelligence and fashioning his thoughts to fruitful issues. Such is the conscious master, and man can only thus become by discovering within himself the laws of thought. This discovery is totally a matter of application, self-analysis and experience.

Only by much searching and mining are gold and diamonds obtained, and man can find every truth connected with his being, if he will dig deep into the mine of his soul. That he is the maker of his character, the molder of his life, and the builder of his destiny, he may unerringly prove, if he will watch, control, and alter his thoughts, tracing their effects upon himself, upon others and upon his life and circumstances, linking cause and effect by patient practice and investigation. And utilizing his every experience, even the most trivial, everyday occurrence, as a means of obtaining that knowledge of himself which is understanding, wisdom, power. In this direction is the law of absolute that "He that seeketh findeth; and to him that knocketh it shall be opened." For only by patience, practice, and ceaseless importunity can a man enter the door of the temple of knowledge.

THOUGHT AND PURPOSE

Until thought is linked with purpose there is no intelligent accomplishment. With the majority the bark of thought is allowed to "drift" upon the ocean of life. Aimlessness is a vice, and such drifting must not continue for him who would streer clear of catastrophe and destruction.

They who have no central purpose in their life fall an easy prey to petty worries, fears, troubles, and self-pityings, all of which are indications of weakness, which lead, just as surely as deliberately planned sins (though by a different route), to failure, unhappiness, and loss, for weakness cannot persist in a power-evolving universe.

A man should conceive of a legitimate purpose in his heart, and set out to accomplish it. He should make this purpose the centralizing point of his thoughts. It may take the form of a spiritual ideal, or it may be a worldly object, according to his nature at the time being. Whichever it is, he should steadily focus his thought-forces upon the object he had set before him. He should make this purpose his supreme duty and should devote himself to its attainment, not allowing his thoughts to wander away into ephemeral fancies, longings, and imaginings. This is the royal road to self-control and true concentration of thought. Even if he fails again and again to accomplish his purpose—as he must until weakness is overcome—the strength of character gained will be the measure of his true success, and this will form a new starting point for future power and triumph.

Those who are not prepared for the apprehension of a great purpose should fix their thoughts upon the faultless performance of their duty, no matter how insignificant their task may appear. Only in this way can the thoughts be gathered and focused, and resolution and energy be developed. Once this is done, there is nothing which may not be accomplished.

The weakest soul knowing its own weakness, and believing this truth—that strength can only be developed by effort and practice—will, thus believing, at once begin to exert itself. And, adding effort to effort, patience to patience, and strength to strength, will never cease to develop and will at last grow divinely strong.

As the physically weak man can make himself strong by careful and patient training, so the man of weak thoughts can make them strong by exercising himself in right thinking.

To put away aimlessness and weakness and to begin to think with purpose is to enter the ranks of those strong ones who only recognize failure as one of the pathways to attainment. Who make all conditions serve them, and who think strongly, attempt fearlessly, and accomplish masterfully.

Having conceived of his purpose, a man should mentally mark out a straight pathway to its achievement, looking neither to the right nor left. Doubts and fears should be rigorously excluded. They are disintegrating elements which break up the straight line of effort, rendering it crooked, ineffectual, useless. Thoughts of doubt and fear can never accomplish anything. They always lead to failure. Purpose, energy, power to do, and all strong thoughts cease when doubt and fear creep in.

The will to do springs from the knowledge that we can do. Doubt and fear are the great enemies of knowledge, and he who encourages them, who does not slay them, thwarts himself at every step.

He who has conquered doubt and fear has conquered failure. His every thought is allied with power, and all difficulties are bravely met and overcome. His purposes are seasonably planted, and they bloom and bring forth fruit that does not fall prematurely to the ground.

Thought allied fearlessly to purpose becomes creative force. He who knows this is ready to become something higher and stronger than a bundle of wavering thoughts and fluctuating sensations. He who does this has become the conscious and intelligent wielder of his mental powers.

VISIONS AND IDEALS

The dreamers are the saviors of the world. As the visible world is sustained by the invisible, so men, through all their trials and sins and sordid vocations, are nourished by the beautiful visions of their solitary dreamers. Humanity cannot forget its dreamers; it cannot let their ideals fade and die; it lives in them; it knows them as the realities which it shall one day see and know.

Composer, sculptor, painter, poet, prophet, sage—these are the makers of the after-world, the architects of heaven. The world is beautiful because they have lived. Without them, laboring humanity would perish.

He who cherishes a beautiful vision, a lofty ideal in his heart, will one day realize it. Columbus cherished a vision of another world and he discovered it. Copernicus fostered the vision of a multiplicity of worlds and a wider universe, and he revealed it. Buddha beheld the vision of a spiritual world of stainless beauty and perfect peace, and he entered into it.

Cherish your visions; cherish your ideals. Cherish the music that stirs in your heart, the beauty that forms in your mind, the loveliness that drapes your purest thoughts. For out of them will grow all delightful conditions, all heavenly environment; of these, if you but remain true to them, your world will at last be built.

To desire is to obtain; to aspire is to achieve. Shall man's basest desires receive the fullest measure of gratification, and his purest aspirations starve for lack of sustenance? Such is not the Law. Such a condition can never obtain: "Ask and receive."

Dream lofty dreams, and as you dream, so shall you become. Your vision is the promise of what you shall one day be; your ideal is the prophecy of what you shall at last unveil.

The greatest achievement was at first and for a time a dream. The oak sleeps in the acorn; the bird waits in the egg. And in the highest vision of a soul a waking angel stirs. Dreams are the seedlings of realities.

Your circumstances may be uncongenial, but they shall not remain so if you only perceive an ideal and strive to reach it. You can't travel within and stand still without. Here is a youth hard pressed by poverty and labor. Confined long hours in an unhealthy workshop; unschooled and lacking all the arts of refinement. But he dreams of better things. He thinks of intelligence, or refinement, of grace and beauty. He conceives of, mentally builds up, an ideal condition of life. The wider liberty and a larger scope takes possession of him; unrest urges him to action, and he uses all his spare times and means to the development of his latent powers and resources. Very soon so altered has his mind become that the workshop can no longer hold him. It has become so out of harmony with his mind-set that it falls out of his life as a garment is cast aside. And with the growth of opportunities that fit the scope of his expanding powers, he passes out of it altogether.

Years later we see this youth as a grown man. We find him a master of certain forces of the mind that he wields with world-wide influence and almost unequaled power.

In his hands he holds the cords of gigantic responsibilities; he speaks, and lives are changed; men and women hang upon his words and remold their characters. Sun-like, he becomes the fixed and luminous center around which innumerable destinies revolve. He has become the vision of his youth. He has become one with his ideal.

And you too, youthful reader, will realize the vision (not just the idle wish) of your heart, be it base or beautiful, or a mixture of both.

For you will always gravitate toward that which you, secretly, most love. Into your hands will be placed the exact results of your own thoughts;

You will receive that which you earn; no more, no less. Whatever your present environment may be, you will fall, remain, or rise with your thoughts—your vision, your ideal. You will become as small as your controlling desire; as great as your dominant aspiration.

The thoughtless, the ignorant, and the indolent, seeing only the apparent effects of things and not the things themselves, talk of luck, of fortune, and chance. Seeing a man grow rich, they say, "How lucky he is!" Observing another become skilled intellectually, they exclaim, "How highly favored he is!" And noting the saintly character and wide influence of another, they remark, "How chance helps him at every turn!" They do not see the trials and failures and struggles which these men have encountered in order to gain their experience. They have no knowledge of the sacrifices they have made, of the undaunted efforts they have put forth, of the faith they have exercised so that they might overcome the apparently insurmountable and realize the vision of their heart. They do not know the darkness and the heartaches; they only see the light and joy, and call it "luck." Do not see the long, arduous journey, but only behold the pleasant goal and call it "good fortune." Do not understand the process, but only perceive the result, and call it "chance."

In all human affairs there are efforts, and there are results. The strength of the effort is the measure of the result. Change is not. Gifts, powers, material, intellectual, and spiritual possessions are the fruits of effort.

They are thoughts completed, objectives accomplished, visions realized.

The vision that you glorify in your mind, the ideal that you enthrone in your heart—this you will build your life by; this you will become.

Books For Further Reading

Just be reading for 1 hour a day, over a year that's reading for 15 full 24-hour days.

15 full 24-hour days of positive food for your mind.

**Change your thoughts, sell more
Timeshare...................FACT**

Napoleon Hill	*Think and Grow Rich*
Napoleon Hill & W Clement Stone	*Success Through A Positive Mental Attitude*
Napoleon Hill	*Keys to Success*
Dale Carnegie	*How To Win Friends and Influence People*
Dale Carnegie	*How to Stop Worrying and Start Living*
George Clason	*The Richest Man in Babylon*
Joseph Murphy	*The Power of your Subconscious Mind*
Norman Vincent Peale	*The Amazing Results of Positive Thinking*
Norman Vincent Peale	*The Power of Positive Thinking*
D.J. Schwatz	*The Magic of Thinking Big*
M Simmons	*Your Subconscious Power*
W Clement Stone	*The Success System That never Fails*
Ben Sweetland	*I Can*
Ben Sweetland	*I Will*

Ben Sweetland	*Grow Rich While You Sleep*
Jeffrey Gitomer	*Little Green Book of Getting Your Way*
Jeffrey Gitomer	*Little Yellow Book of YES! Attitude*
Jeffrey Gitomer	*Little Red Book of Sales Answers*
Jeffrey Gitomer	*Customer Satisfaction is Worthless, Customer Loyalty is Priceless*
O G Mandino	*The Greatest Salesman In The World*

TESTIMONALS

Dear Carl Garwood

I thought I would write this as I felt you should know that you are the only one who has given me inspiration and belief in myself. Since meeting you my sales have been taken to a different level. I put it down to whatever my mind can conceive and believe I will achieve. I wish you and your beautiful family all the best.

Matthew Alwright

I started the programme at 11% closing. I have been working in sales for almost 10 months and never reached higher that 13% closing.

Carl devised a programme of positive thinking, goal setting and focus.

I had a new goal – to be 25% net closing – year to date.

I re-focused my goals and read them with passion each morning and evening. I devised some self motivating affirmations and read positive attitude books. We discussed the week every Monday and altered the programme accordingly.

At the end of the first month I closed a net 25% First time ever!!! The next month was a little harder – as the momentum wore off I was letting the Negative side creep in. Carl took me aside and re-focused the goals and set me back on the right track.

I finished the month closing at 25% - the YTD figure was 21%. Which is a fantastic achievement.

I now know that I am in control over my attitude and my life!!! I am learning to accept rejection and count it as a step closer to success. I have raised my goals this month and will apply everything I have learned to succeed.

Not only has this course changed me at work – it has also vastly improved my personal life.

Thank you Carl, I will never underestimate the power of positive thinking and goal setting. You have changed my life for the better.

Julie Burgess

I have recently finished my coaching period with Carl and it has made a tremendous difference not only in my work time but also in my private life as well. I have always had belief in myself but Carl took that to another level and I have now almost doubled in my closing percentages. Carl helped me home in on my skills which I honestly believe has made a huge impact in the way I now go about my business and I can not thank him enough for what he has done for me. Anyone who is thinking of taking on coaching with Carl my advice is *Just do it* you certainly will not regret it.

Thank you Carl

Daniel Drake

Hi Carl

I also want to say a big Thank You for your support, help and encouragement in the last two periods. I thoroughly enjoyed having you as my Coach and certainly got a lot from it. I felt as lot more focused and inspired having set a goal of 25% closing to aim for each month. First period was amazing and I succeeded in obtaining that closing and second although not as good, I still benefited from your support. It was a tough month for me on a personal front and although I tried to keep it away from work, I guess somehow sub-consciously it still affects you. What I do know is that without your support and focus, it may have been worse. It's amazing how much one can succeed with stringent goals, a definite major purpose and above all belief. I will certainly adopt the same theory to the rest of my year and aim to be in the top 3 by the end of 2006.

Once again I'm very grateful to have had this rare opportunity with you and know that you will succeed in your purpose with all future candidates.

Margaret Lopes

Carl Garwood is The Timeshare Coach[SM] A certified instructor for the Napoleon Hill foundation, author and motivational speaker. The Timeshare Coach[SM] brings 13 years of experience in the Timeshare industry as a Sales Professional, Sales Team Leader, Sales Manager, Podium Presenter and Sales Trainer.

The Timeshare Coach[SM] is your strongest believer. He will show you the best in yourself and help you achieve more sales. The Timeshare Coach[SM] will give you direction, put purpose in your stride, strengthen your will and give you unquestionable belief. He is your own personal coach.

For more details on personal coaching, sales training and motivational Timeshare seminars contact sales@ thetimesharecoach.com or visit www.thetimesharecoach.com

KRS1

CPSIA information can be obtained at www.ICGtesting.com
Printed in the USA
BVOW08s0657250716

456585BV00001BA/17/P